INDIVIDUALISM OLD AND NEW

INDIVIDUALISM OLD AND NEW

COMMON FAITH

LIBRALISM AND SOCIAL ACTION

By John Dewey

ISBN 1934568507

Frederick Ellis, Publisher
6015 S. Virginia, Suite E365
Reno, Nevada 89502

Contents

1. THE HOUSE DIVIDED AGAINST ITSELF

It is becoming a commonplace to say that in thought and feeling, or at least in the language in which they are expressed, we are living in some bygone century, anywhere from the thirteenth to the eighteenth, although physically and externally we belong to the twentieth century. In such a contradictory condition, it is not surprising that a report of American life, such as is contained, for example, in *Middletown*, should frequently refer to a "bewildered" or "confused" state of mind as characteristic of us.

Anthropologically speaking, we are living in a money culture. Its cult and rites dominate. "The money medium of exchange and the cluster of activities associated with its acquisition drastically condition the other activities of the people." This, of course, is as it should be; people have to make a living, do they not? And for what should they work if not for money, and how should they get goods and enjoyments if not by buying them with money—thus enabling someone else to make more money, and in the end to start shops and factories to give employment to still others, so that they can make more money to enable other people to make more money by selling goods—and so on indefinitely. So far, all is for the best in the best of all possible cultures: our rugged—or is it ragged?—individualism.

And if the culture pattern works out so that society is divided into two classes, the working group and the business (including professional) group, with two and a half times as many in the former as in the latter, and with the chief ambition of parents in the former class that their children should climb into the latter, that is doubtless because American life offers such unparalleled opportunities for each individual to prosper according to his virtues. If few workers know what they are making or the meaning of what they do, and still fewer know what becomes of the work of their hands—in the largest industry of Middletown perhaps one-tenth of one percent of the product is consumed locally—this is doubtless because we have so perfected our system of distribution that the whole country is one. And if the mass of workers live in constant fear of loss of their jobs, this is doubtless because our spirit of progress, manifest in change of fashions, invention of new machines and power of overproduction, keeps everything on the move. Our reward of industry and thrift is so accurately adjusted to individual ability that it is natural and proper that the workers should look forward with dread to the age of fifty or fifty-five, when they will be laid on the shelf.

All this we take for granted; it is treated as an inevitable part of our social system. To dwell on the dark side of it is to blaspheme against our religion of prosperity. But it is a system that calls for a hard and strenuous philosophy. If one looks at what we do and what happens, and then expects to find a theory of life that harmonizes with the actual situation, he will be shocked by the contradiction he comes upon. For the situation calls for assertion of complete economic determinism. We live as if economic forces determined the growth and decay of institutions and settled the fate of individuals. Liberty becomes a well-nigh obsolete term; we start, go, and stop at the signal of a vast industrial machine. Again, the actual system would seem to imply a pretty definitely materialistic scheme of value. Worth is measured by ability to hold one's own or to get ahead in a competitive pecuniary race. "Within the privacy of shabby or ambitious houses, marriage, birth, child-rearing, death, and the personal immensities of family life go forward. However, it is not so much these functional urgencies of life that determine how favorable this physical necessity shall be, but the extraneous detail of how much money the father earns." The philosophy appropriate to such a situation is that of struggle for existence and survival of the economically fit. One would expect the current theory of life, if it reflects the actual situation, to be the most drastic Darwinism. And, finally, one would anticipate that the personal traits most prized would be clear-sighted vision of personal advantage and resolute ambition to secure it at any human cost. Sentiment and sympathy would be at the lowest discount.

It is unnecessary to say that the current view of life in Middle-town, in Anytown, is nothing of this sort. Nothing gives us Americans the horrors more than to hear that some misguided creature in some low part of the earth preaches what we prac-tise—and practise much more efficiently than anyone else—namely, economic determinism. Our whole theory is that man plans and uses machines for his own humane and moral pur-poses, instead of being borne wherever the machine carries him. Instead of materialism, our idealism is probably the loudest and most frequently professed philosophy the world has ever heard. We praise even our most successful men, not for their ruthless and self-centered energy in getting ahead, but because of their love of flowers, children, and dogs, or their kindness to aged relatives. Anyone who frankly urges a selfish creed of life is everywhere frowned upon. Along with the disappearance of the home, and the multiplication of divorce in one generation by 600 percent, there is the most abundant and most sentimental glorification of the sacredness of home and the beauties of con-stant love that history can record. We are surcharged with altru-ism and bursting with desire to "serve" others.

These are only a few of the obvious contradictions between our institutions and practice on one hand, and our creeds and theories on the other, contradictions which a survey of any of our Middletowns reveals. It is not surprising that the inhabitants of these towns are bewildered, uneasy, restless, always seeking something new and different, only to find, as a rule, the same old thing in a new dress. It may all be summed up, perhaps, by say-ing that nowhere in the world at any time has religion been so thoroughly respectable as with us, and so nearly totally discon-nected from life. I hesitate to dwell on the revelation that this book gives of "religious" life in Middletown. The glorification of religion as setting the final seal of approval on pecuniary success, and supplying the active motive to more energetic struggle for such success, and the adoption by the churches of the latest devices of the movies and the advertiser, approach too close to the obscene. Schooling is developed to the point where more pupils reach the high school than in other lands; and one-half of the pupils in the last years of the high school think that the first chapters of the Hebrew Scriptures give a more accurate account of the origin and early history of man than does science, and only one-fifth actively dissent. If the investigation had been made when a certain questionnaire was distributed among our school children, it is likely that the usual percentage of youth would have recorded their belief that Harding was the greatest man in the world. In another way, the whole story is told in brief when one contrasts what is actually happening to family life and the complete secularization of daily activities with a statement from the pulpit that "the three notable words in the English language are mother, home and heaven," a remark that would certainly pass unquestioned in any representative American audience.

It makes little difference whether one selects important or trivial aspects of the contradiction between our life as we outwardly live it and our thoughts and feelings—or what we at least say are our beliefs and sentiments. The significant question is: What is the cause of this split and contradiction? There are those, of course, who attribute it to the fact that people being, generally speaking, morons and boobs, they must be expected to act out the parts to which they are assigned. The "explanation" does not take us very far, even if one accepts it. The particular forms that the alleged boobery takes are left quite unaccounted for. And the more one knows of history, the more one comes to believe that traditions and institutions count more than native capacity or incapacity in explaining things. It is evident enough that the rapid industrialization of our civilization took us unawares. Being mentally and morally unprepared, our older creeds have become ingrowing; the more we depart from them in fact, the more loudly we proclaim them. In effect we treat them as magic formulae. By repeating them often enough we hope to ward off the evils of the new situation, or at least to prevent ourselves from seeing them—and this latter function is ably performed by our nominal beliefs.

With an enormous command of instrumentalities, with possession of a secure technology, we glorify the past, and legalize and idealize the *status quo*, instead of seriously asking how we are to employ the means at our disposal so as to form an equitable and stable society. This is our great abdication. It explains how and why we are a house divided against itself. Our tradition, our heritage, is itself double. It contains in itself the ideal of equality of opportunity and of freedom for all, without regard to birth and status, as a condition for the effective realization of that equality. This ideal and endeavor in its behalf once constituted our essential Americanism; that which was prized as the note of a new world. It is the genuinely spiritual element of our tradition. No one can truthfully say that it has entirely disappeared. But its promise of a new moral and religious outlook has not been attained. It has not become the well-spring of a new intellectual consensus; it is not (even unconsciously) the vital source of any distinctive and shared philosophy. It directs our politics only spasmodically, and while it has generously provided schools it does not control their aims or their methods.

Meanwhile our institutions embody another and older tradition. Industry and business conducted for money profit are nothing new; they are not the product of our own age and culture; they come to us from a long past. But the invention of the machine has given them a power and scope they never had in the past from which they derive. Our law and politics and the incidents of human association depend upon a novel combination of the machine and money, and the result is the pecuniary culture characteristic of our civilization. The spiritual factor of our tradition, equal opportunity and free association and intercommunication, is obscured and crowded out. Instead of the development of individualities which it prophetically set forth, there is a perversion of the whole ideal of individualism to conform to the practices of a pecuniary culture. It has become the source and justification of inequalities and oppressions. Hence our compromises, and the conflicts in which aims and standards are confused beyond recognition.

2. AMERICA.....BY FORMULA

We have heard a good deal of late years of class-consciousness. The phrase "nation-conscious" does not happen to be current, but present-day nationalism is an exacerbated expression of it in fact. A still more recent manifestation might be called "culture-consciousness" or "civilization-consciousness." Like class-consciousness and nationalism, it assumes an invidious form; it is an exponent—and a coefficient—of conflict between groups. The war and its consequences may not have produced in our own country a consciousness of "Americanism" as a distinctive mode of civilization but they have definitely had that effect among the intellectual elite of Europe.

Americanism as a form of culture did not exist, before the war, for Europeans. Now it does exist and as a menace. In reaction and as a protest, there is developing, at least among literary folk, the consciousness of a culture which is distinctively European, something which is precious and whose very existence is threatened by an invasion of a new form of barbarism issuing from the United States. Acute hostility to a powerful alien influence is taking the place of complacent ignoring of what was felt to be negligible. It would take a wider knowledge than mine to list even the titles of books and articles coming yearly from the presses of Europe whose burden is the threat of "America" to the traditional culture of Europe.

I am not concerned here with the European side of the matter. Most social unifications come about in response to external pressure. The same is likely to be true of a United States of Europe. If the ideal is approximated in reality, it will probably be as a protective reaction to the economic and financial hegemony of the United States of America. The result would probably be a good thing for Europe, and thus unwittingly we should serve one good purpose, internationally speaking. But it is, in the end, no great consolation to know that in losing our own soul we have been a means of helping save the soul of some one else. Just what is the America whose picture is forming in the minds of European critics?

Some of the writers are ignorant as well as bitter. These may be neglected. Others are intelligent, as well-informed as any foreigner can be about a foreign country, and not devoid of sympathy. Moreover their judgments agree not only with one another but with the protests of native-born dissenters. For convenience and because of the straightforward intelligence of its author, I take as a point of departure, the description of the American type of mind and character presented by Mueller Freienfels.[1] His treatment is the fairer because he understands by "American" a type of mind that is developing, from like causes, all over the world, and which would have emerged in time in Europe, even if there were no geographical America, although its development in the rest of the world has been accelerated and intensified by the influence of this country.

As far as any actual American is true to the type that is proclaimed to be *the* American, he should be thrilled by the picture that is drawn of him. For we are told that the type is a genuine mutation in the history of culture; that it is new, the product of the last century, and that it is stamped with success. It is transforming the external conditions of life and thereby reacting on the psychical content of life; it is assimilating other types of itself and re-coining them. No world-conquest, whether that of Rome or Christendom, compares with that of "Americanism" in extent or effectiveness. If success and quantity are in fact the standards of the "American," here are admissions that will content his soul. From the standpoint of the type depicted, he is approved; and what do adverse criticisms matter?

But either the type is not yet so definitely fixed as is represented, or else there are individual Americans who deviate from type. For there are many who will have reserves in their admiration of the picture that is presented. Of course the dissenters may be, as the European critics say, impotent sports, fish out of water and affected with nostalgia for the European tradition. Nevertheless, it is worth while to raise the question as to whether the American type, supposing there is to be one, has as yet taken on definitive form. First, however, what are alleged to be the characteristics of the type?

Fundamentally, they spring from impersonality. The roots of the intellect are unconscious and vital, in instincts and emotions. In America, we are told, this subconsciousness is disregarded; it is suppressed or is subordinated to conscious rationality, which means that it is adapted to the needs and conditions of the external world. We have "intellect," but distinctly in the Bergsonian sense; mind attuned to the conditions of action upon matter, upon the world. Our emotional life is quick, excitable, undiscriminating, lacking in individuality and in direction by intellectual life. Hence the "externality and superficiality of the American soul"; it has no ultimate inner unity and uniqueness—no true personality.

The marks and signs of this "impersonalization" of the human soul are quantification of life, with its attendant disregard of quality; its mechanization and the almost universal habit of esteeming technique as an end, not as a means, so that organic and intellectual life is also "rationalized"; and, finally, standardization. Differences and distinctions are ignored and overridden; agreement, similarity, is the ideal. There is not only absence of social discrimination but of intellectual; critical thinking is conspicuous by its absence. Our pronounced trait is mass suggestibility. The adaptability and flexibility that we display in our practical intelligence when dealing with external conditions have found their way into our souls. Homogeneity of thought and emotion has become an ideal.

Quantification, mechanization and standardization: these are then the marks of the Americanization that is conquering the world. They have their good side; external conditions and the standard of living are undoubtedly improved. But their effects are not limited to these matters; they have invaded mind and character, and subdued the soul to their own dye. The criticism is familiar; it is so much the burden of our own critics that one is never quite sure how much of the picture of foreign critics is drawn from direct observation and how much from native novels and essays that are not complacent with the American scene. This fact does not detract from the force of the indictment; it rather adds to it, and raises the more insistently the question of what our life means.

I shall not deny the existence of these characteristics, nor of the manifold evils of superficialism and externalism that result in the production of intellectual and moral mediocrity. In the main these traits exist and they characterize American life and are already beginning to dominate that of other countries. But their import is another thing than their existence. Mueller Freienfels is intelligent enough to acknowledge that they are transitional rather than final. He recognizes that the forces are so intrinsic that it is foolish to rebel against them and lament the past. "The question is how we are to pass through them and transcend them." It is this note which distinguishes his appraisal from so many others.

In reply to the question, one may at least say that we are still in an early stage of the transition. Anything that is at most but a hundred years old has hardly had time to disclose its meaning in the slow secular processes of human history. And it may be questioned whether even our author has not sometimes succumbed to the weakness of lesser critics in treating the passing symptoms as inherent characters. I do not have in mind here an "optimistic" appeal to future time and its possibilities. I rather wish to raise the question as to how many of the defects and evils that are supposed to belong to the present order are in fact projections into it of a departing past order.

Strength, power, is always relative, not absolute. Conquest is an exhibition of weakness in the conquered as well as of strength in the conqueror. Transitions are out of something as well as into something; they reveal a past as well as project a future. There must have been something profoundly awry in the quality, spirituality and individualized variety of the past, or they would not have succumbed as readily as we are told they are doing to the quantification, mechanization and standardization of the present. And the defective and perverse elements have certainly not been displaced. They survive in the present. Present conditions give these factors an opportunity to disclose themselves. They are not now kept under and out of sight. Their overt manifestation is not a cheering spectacle. But as long as they did not show themselves on a scale large enough to attract notice, they could not be dealt with. I wonder very much whether many of the things that are objected to in the present scene—and justly so— are not in fact revelations of what the older type of culture covered up, and whether their perceptible presence is not to be credited rather than debited to the forces that are now active.

It is possible of course to argue—as Keyserling for example seems to do—that the new or American order signifies simply that the animal instincts of man have been released, while the older European tradition kept them in disciplined subjection to something higher, called with pleasing vagueness "spirituality." The suspicion that suppression is not solution is not confined to America. Undue and indiscriminate greediness in the presence of accessible food may be a symptom of previous starvation rather than an inevitable exhibition of the old Adam. A culture whose tradition rests on depreciation of the flesh and on making a sharp difference between body and mind, instinct and reason, practice and theory, may have wrought corruption of flesh and degeneration of spirit. It would take a degree of wisdom no one possesses to tell just what, in the undesirable features of the present, is a reflection of an old but not as yet transformed system of life and thought, and how much is a genuine product of the new forces.

One thing seems to be reasonably certain. The prized and vaunted "individuality" of European culture that is threatened by the leveling standardization and uniformity of the American type was a very limited affair. If one were to retort in kind, one could ask how much share in it was had by the peasant and proletarian. And it is much more than a retort to say that a peasantry and proletariat which has been released from intellectual bondage will for a time have its revenge. Because there is no magic in democracy to confer immediately the power of critical discrimination upon the masses who have been outside any intellectual movement, and who have taken their morals and their religion from an external authority above them—an authority which science is destroying—it does not follow that the ineptitude of the many is the creation of democracy.

Take one instance—the present interest in technique, and the domination of the "American type" by technique. It will hardly be argued I suppose that the mere absence of technique—intelligent means and methods for securing results—is itself a mark of an intrinsically desirable civilization. Nor is it surprising that the discovery of the actuality and potentiality of technique in all branches of human life should have an immediately intoxicating effect. What is called the American mentality is characterized by this discovery, and by the exaggerations that come with the abruptness of the discovery. There is much to be said against quantification and standardization. But the discovery of competent technique stands on a different level. The world has not suffered from absence of ideals and spiritual aims anywhere nearly as much as it has suffered from absence of means for realizing the ends which it has prized in a literary and sentimental way. Technique is still a novelty in most matters, and like most novelties is played with for a while on its own account. But it will be used for ends beyond itself sometime; and I think that interest in technique is precisely the thing which is most promising in our civilization, the thing which in the end will break down devotion to external standardization and the mass-quantity ideal. For its application has not gone far as yet; and interest in it is still largely vicarious, being that, so to say, of the spectator rather than of naturalization in use. In the end, technique can only signify emancipation of individuality, and emancipation on a broader scale than has obtained in the past.

In his most hopeful anticipation of a future to which we may be moving, Freienfels calls attention to the fact that the impoverishment of the individual is accompanied, even now, by an enrichment of community resources. Collectively, present society, he says, is marked by a power over nature and by intellectual resource and power exceeding that of the classic Athenian and the man of the Renaissance. Why is it that this collective enrichment does not operate to elevate correspondingly the life of individuals? This question he does not ask. Failure to consider it constitutes to my mind the chief failure of critics whether foreign or native. Our materialism, our devotion to money making and to having a good time are not things by themselves. They are the product of the fact that we live in a money culture; of the fact that our technique and technology are controlled by interest in private profit. There lies the serious and fundamental defect of our civilization, the source of the secondary and induced evils to

which so much attention is given. Critics are dealing with symptoms and effects. The evasion of fundamental economic causes
by critics both foreign and native seems to me to be an indication
of the prevalence of the old European tradition, with its disregard for the body, material things and practical concerns. The
development of the American type, in the sense of the critics, is
an expression of the fact that we have retained this tradition and
the economic system of private gain on which it is based, while at
the same time we have made an independent development of
industry and technology that is nothing short of revolutionary.
When our critics deal with this issue instead of avoiding it there
will be something really doing.

Until the issue is met, the confusion of a civilization divided
against itself will persist. The mass development, which our European critics tell us has submerged individuality, *is* the product of
a machine age; in some form it will follow in all countries from
the extension of a machine technology. Its immediate effect has
been, without doubt, a subjection of certain types of individuality. As far as individuality is associated with aristocracy of the
historic type, the extension of the machine age will presumably
be hostile to individuality in its traditional sense all over the
world. But the strictures of our European critics only define the
issue touched upon in the previous chapter. The problem of constructing a new individuality consonant with the objective conditions under which we live is the deepest problem of our times.

There are two "solutions" that fail to solve. One of these is the
method of avoidance. This course is taken as far as it is assumed
that the only valid type of individuality is that which holds over
from the ages that anteceded machine technology and the democratic society it creates. The course that is complementary to the
method of escape springs from assumption that the present situation is final; that it presents something inherently ultimate and
fixed. Only as it is treated as transitive and moving, as material
to be dealt with in shaping a later outcome, only, that is, as it is
treated as a *problem*, is the idea of any solution genuine and relevant. We may well take the formula advanced by European critics as a means of developing our consciousness of some of the
conditions of the problem. So regarded, the problem is seen to be
essentially that of creation of a new individualism as significant
for modern conditions as the old individualism at its best was for

its day and place. The first step in furtner definition of this problem is realization of the collective age which we have already entered. When that is apprehended, the issue will define itself as utilization of the realities of a corporate civilization to validate and embody the distinctive moral element in the American version of individualism: Equality and freedom expressed not merely externally and politically but through personal participation in the development of a shared culture.

3. THE UNITED STATES.....INCORPORATED

It was not long ago that it was fashionable for both American and foreign observers of our national scene to sum up the phenomena of our social·life under the title of "individualism." Some treated this alleged individualism as our distinctive achievement; some critics held that it was the source of our backwardness, the mark of a relatively uncivilized estate. To-day both interpretations seem equally inept and outmoded. Individualism is still carried on our banners and attempts are made to use it as a war-cry, especially when it is desired to defeat governmental regulation of any form of industry previously exempt from legal control. Even in high quarters, rugged individualism is praised as the glory of American life. But such words have little relation to the moving facts of that life.

. There is no word which adequately expresses what is taking place. "᠁ocialism" has too specific political and economic associations to be appropriate. "Collectivism" is more neutral, but it, too, is a party-word rather than a descriptive term. Perhaps the constantly increasing role of corporations in our economic life gives a clue to a fitting name. The word may be used in a wider sense than is conveyed by its technical legal meaning. We may then say that the United States has steadily moved from an earlier pioneer individualism to a condition of dominant corporateness. The influence business corporations exercise in determining present industrial and economic activities is both a cause and a symbol of the tendency to combination in all phases of life. Associations tightly or loosely organized more and more define the opportunities, the choices and the actions of individuals.

I have said that the growth of legal corporations in manufacturing, transportation, distribution and finance is symbolic of the development of corporateness in all phases of life. The era of trust-busting is an almost forgotten age. Not only are big mergers the order of the day, but popular sentiment now looks upon them with pride rather than with fear. Size is our current measure of greatness in this as in other matters. It is not necessary to ask whether the opportunity for speculative manipulation for the sake of private gain, or increased public service at a lower cost, is the dominant motive. Personal motives hardly count as productive causes in comparison with impersonal forces. Mass production and mass distribution inevitably follow in the wake of an epoch of steam and electricity. These have created a common market, the parts of which are held together by intercommunication and interdependence; distance is eliminated and the tempo of action enormously accelerated. Aggregated capital and concentrated control are the contemporary responses.

Political control is needed, but the movement cannot be arrested by legislation. Witness the condition of nearly innocuous desuetude of the Sherman Anti-Trust Act. Newspapers, manufacturing plants, utilities supplying light, power and local transportation, banks, retail stores, theaters and the movies, have all joined in the movement toward integration. General Motors, the American Telegraph and Telephone Company, United States Steel, the rapid growth of chain-store systems, combinations of radio companies with companies controlling theaters all over the country, are familiar facts. Railway consolidations have been slowed up by politics and internal difficulties, but few persons doubt that they, too, are coming. The political control of the future to be effective must take a positive instead of negative form.

For the forces at work in this movement are too vast and complex to cease operation at the behest of legislation. Aside from direct evasions of laws, there are many legal methods of carrying the movement forward. Interlocking directorates, interpurchase of stocks by individuals and corporations, grouping into holding companies, investing companies with enough holdings to sway policies, effect the same end as do direct mergers. It was stated at a recent convention of bankers that eighty per cent of the capitalization of all the banks of the country is now in the hands of twelve financial concerns. It is evident that virtual control of the other twenty per cent, except for negligible institutions having only local importance, automatically ensues.

An economist could multiply instances and give them a more precise form. But I am not an economist, and the facts in any case are too well known to need detailed rehearsal. For my purpose is only to indicate the bearing of the development of these corporations upon the change of social life from an individual to a corporate affair. Reactions to the change are psychological, professional, political; they affect the working ideas, beliefs and conduct of all of us.

The sad decline of the farmer cannot be understood except in the light of the industrialization of the country which is coincident with its "corporization." The government is now going to try to do for the collectivizing of the agriculturists the sort of thing that business acumen has already done—temporarily against the desire of the government—for manufactures and transportation. The plight of the uncombined and unintegrated is proof of the extent to which the country is controlled by the corporate idea. Sociologists who concern themselves with rural life are now chiefly occupied with pointing out the influence of urban districts—that is, of those where industrial organization predominates—upon the determination of conditions in country districts.

There are other decays which tell the same story. The old-type artisan, trained by individual apprenticeship for skilled individual work, is disappearing. Mass production by men massed together to operate machines with their minute divisions of labor, is putting him out of business. In many cases, a few weeks at a machine give about all the education—or rather training— that is needed. Mass production causes a kind of mass education in which individual capacity and skill are submerged. While the artisan becomes more of a mechanic and less of an artist, those who are still called artists either put themselves, as writers and designers, at the disposal of organized business, or are pushed out to the edge as eccentric bohemians. The artist remains, one may say, as a surviving individual force, but the esteem in which the calling is socially held in this country measures the degree of his force. The status of the artist in any form of social life affords a fair measure of the state of its culture. The inorganic position of the artist in American life to-day is convincing evidence of what happens to the isolated individual who lives in a society growing corporate.

Attention has recently been called to a new phenomenon in human culture:—the business mind, having its own conversation and language, its own interests, its own intimate groupings in which men of this mind, in their collective capacity, determine the tone of society at large as well as the government of industrial society, and have more political influence than the government itself. I am not concerned here with their political power. The fact significant for present discussion, is that we now have, although without formal or legal status, a mental and moral corporateness for which history affords no parallel. Our indigenous heroes are the Fords and Edisons who typify this mind to the public. Critics may find amusement in ridiculing Rotarians, Kiwanians and Lions, but the latter can well afford to disregard the ridicule because they are representatives of the dominant corporate mentality.

Nowhere is the decline of the old-fashioned individual and individualism more marked than in leisure life, in amusements and sports. Our colleges only follow the movement of the day when they make athletics an organized business, aroused and conducted under paid directors in the spirit of pure collectivism. The formation of theater chains is at once the cause and the effect of the destruction of the older independent life of leisure carried on in separate homes. The radio, the movies, the motor car, all make for a common and aggregate mental and emotional life. With technical exceptions, to be found in special publications and in some portion of all newspapers, the press is the organ of amusement for a hurried leisure time, and it reflects and carries further the formation of mental collectivism by massed methods. Crime, too, is assuming a new form; it is organized and corporate.

Our apartments and our subways are signs of the invasion and decline of privacy. Private "rights" have almost ceased to have a definable meaning. We live exposed to the greatest flood of mass suggestion that any people has ever experienced. The need for united action, and the supposed need of integrated opinion and sentiment, are met by organized propaganda and advertising. The publicity agent is perhaps the most significant symbol of our present social life. There are individuals who resist; but for a time at least, sentiment can be manufactured by mass methods for almost any person or any cause.

These things are not said to be deplored, nor even in order to weigh their merits and demerits. They are merely reported as indications of the nature of our social scene, of the extent to which it is formed and directed by corporate and collective factors toward collective ends. Coincident with these changes in mentality and prestige are basic, if hardly acknowledged, changes in the ideas by which life is interpreted. Industry, again, provides the striking symbols.

What has become of the old-fashioned ideal of thrift? Societies for the promotion of savings among the young were much hurt in their feelings when Henry Ford urged a free scale of expenditures instead of a close scale of personal savings. But his recommendation was in line with all the economic tendencies of the day. Speeded-up mass production demands increased buying. It is promoted by advertising on a vast scale, by instalment selling, by agents skilled in breaking down sales resistance. Hence buying becomes an economic "duty" which is as consonant with the present epoch as thrift was with the period of individualism. For the industrial mechanism depends upon maintaining some kind of an equilibrium between production and consumption. If the equilibrium is disturbed, the whole social structure is affected and prosperity ceases to have a meaning. Replacement and extension of capital are indeed more required than they ever were. But the savings of individuals, as such, are petty and inadequate to the task. New capital is chiefly supplied by the surplus earnings of big corporate organizations, and it becomes meaningless to tell individual buyers that industry can be kept going only by their abstinence from the enjoyments of consumption. The old plea for "sacrifice" loses its force. In effect, the individual is told that by indulging in the enjoyment of free purchasing he performs his economic duty, transferring his surplus income to the corporate store where it can be most effectively used. Virtue departs from mere thrift.

The corresponding change in the ruling conceptions of the older economic theory is, of course, the obligation upon employers to pay high wages. Growing consumption through increased expenditure that effects a still greater amount of production cannot be maintained unless consumers have the wherewithal. The consumption demand of the well-to-do is limited; and their number is limited. Purchase of luxuries by this class has, indeed, become a necessity rather than a vice, since it helps to keep moving the wheels of industry and commerce. Luxury may still be condemned as a vice, just as old habits still show themselves in approving thrift as a virtue. But the condemnation is almost an idle beating of the air, because it goes contrary to the movement of industry and trade. In any case, however, there is a definite limit to the consumption of luxuries, as well as of what used to be called necessary commodities, on the part of the wealthy. The demands that make production and distribution "going concerns" must come from the mass of the people, that is, from workers and those in subordinate salaried positions. Hence the "new economy" based on the idea of the identity of high wages with industrial prosperity.

It is difficult, perhaps impossible, to measure the full import of this revaluation of those concepts of saving and low wages which were basic in the older doctrine. If it merely expressed a change in abstract economic theory, its significance would not be great. But the change in theory is itself a reflex of a social change, which is hardly less than revolutionary. I do not mean that I think that the "new economy" is firmly established as a fact, or that the endless chain of speeding up mass consumption in order to speed up production is either endless or entirely logical. But certain changes do not go backward. Those who have enjoyed high wages and a higher standard of consumption will not be content to return to a lower level. A new condition has been created with which we shall have to reckon constantly in the future. Depressions and slumps will come, but they can never be treated in the future in the casual and fatalistic way in which they have been accepted in the past. They will appear abnormal instead of normal, and society, including the industrial captains, will have to assume a responsibility from which it and they were previously exempt. The gospel of general prosperity in this life will have to meet tests to which that of salvation in the next world, as a compensation for the miseries of this one, was not subjected. "Prosperity" is not such an assured fact in 1930 as it seemed to many to be in the earlier part of 1929. The slump or the depression makes the problem caused by the growth of corporate industry and finance the more acute. An excess income of eight billions a year will only aggravate the economic situation unless it can find outlet in productive channels. It cannot do this unless consumption is sustained. This cannot happen unless organization and control extend from production and distribution to consumption. The alternatives seem to be either a definite expansion of social corporateness to include the average consumer or else economic suffering on a vast scale.

I have said that the instances cited of the reaction of the growing corporateness of society upon social mind and habit were not given in order to be either deplored or approved. They are set forth only to call out the picture of the decline of an individualistic philosophy of life, and the formation of a collectivistic scheme of interdependence, which finds its way into every cranny of life, personal, intellectual, emotional, affecting leisure as well as work, morals as well as economics. But because the purpose was to indicate the decay of the older conceptions, although they are still those that are most loudly and vocally professed, the illustrations given inevitably emphasize those features of growing standardization and mass uniformity which critics justly deplore. It would be unfair, accordingly, to leave the impression that these traits are the whole of the story of the "corporization" of American life.

The things which are criticized are the outward signs of an inner movement toward integration on a scale never known before. "Socialization" is not wholly a eulogistic term nor a desirable process. It involves danger to some precious values; it involves a threat of danger to some things which we should not readily lose. But in spite of much cant which is talked about "service" and "social responsibility," it marks the beginning of a new era of integration. What its ultimate possibilities are, and to what extent these possibilities will be realized, is for the future to tell. The need of the present is to apprehend the fact that, for better or worse, we are living in a corporate age.

It is of the nature of society as of life to contain a balance of opposed forces. Actions and reactions are ultimately equal and counterpart. At present the "socialization" is largely mechanical and quantitative. The system is kept in a kind of precarious balance by the movement toward lawless and reckless overstimulation among individuals. If the chaos and the mechanism are to generate a mind and soul, an integrated personality, it will have to be an intelligence, a sentiment and an individuality of a new type.

Meanwhile, the lawlessness and irregularity (and I have in mind not so much outward criminality as emotional instability and intellectual confusion) and the uniform standardization are two sides of the same emerging corporate society. Hence only in an external sense does society maintain a balance. When the corporateness becomes internal, when, that is, it is realized in thought and purpose, it will become qualitative. In this change, law will be realized not as a rule arbitrarily imposed from without but as the relations which hold individuals together. The balance of the individual and the social will be organic. The emotions will be aroused and satisfied in the course of normal living, not in abrupt deviations to secure the fulfillment which is denied them in a situation which is so incomplete that it cannot be admitted into the affections and yet is so pervasive that it cannot be escaped: a situation which defines an individual divided within himself.

4. THE LOST INDIVIDUAL

The development of a civilization that is outwardly corporate—or rapidly becoming so—has been accompanied by a
submergence of the individual. Just how far this is true of the
individual's opportunities in action, how far initiative and choice
in what an individual does are restricted by the economic forces
that make for consolidation, I shall not attempt to say. It is argu-
able that there has been a diminution of the range of decision
and activity for the many along with exaggeration of opportunity of personal expression for the few. It may be contended
that no one class in the past has the power now possessed by an
industrial oligarchy. On the other hand, it may be held that this
power of the few is, with respect to genuine individuality, specious; that those outwardly in control are in reality as much carried by forces external to themselves as are the many; that in fact
these forces impel them into a common mold to such an extent
that individuality is suppressed.

What is here meant by "the lost individual" is, however, so
irrelevant to this question that it is not necessary to decide
between the two views. For by it is meant a moral and intellectual fact which is independent of any manifestation of power in
action. The significant thing is that the loyalties which once held
individuals, which gave them support, direction and unity of
outlook on life, have well-nigh disappeared. In consequence,
individuals are confused and bewildered. It would be difficult to
find in history an epoch as lacking in solid and assured objects of
belief and approved ends of action as is the present. Stability of
individuality is dependent upon stable objects to which allegiance firmly attaches itself. There are, of course, those who are

still militantly fundamentalist in religious and social creed. But their very clamor is evidence that the tide is set against them. For the others, traditional objects of loyalty have become hollow or are openly repudiated, and they drift without sure anchorage. Individuals vibrate between a past that is intellectually too empty to give stability and a present that is too diversely crowded and chaotic to afford balance or direction to ideas and emotion.

Assured and integrated individuality is the product of definite social relationships and publicly acknowledged functions. Judged by this standard, even those who seem to be in control, and to carry the expression of their special individual abilities to a high pitch, are submerged. They may be captains of finance and industry, but until there is some consensus of belief as to the meaning of finance and industry in civilization as a whole, they cannot be captains of their own souls—their beliefs and aims. They exercise leadership surreptitiously and, as it were, absent-mindedly. They lead, but it is under cover of impersonal and socially undirected economic forces. Their reward is found not in what they do, in their social office and function, but in a deflection of social consequences to private gain. They receive the acclaim and command the envy and admiration of the crowd, but the crowd is also composed of private individuals who are equally lost to a sense of social bearings and uses.

The explanation is found in the fact that while the actions promote corporate and collective results, these results are outside their intent and irrelevant to that reward of satisfaction which comes from a sense of social fulfillment. To themselves and to others, their business is private and its outcome is private profit. No complete satisfaction is possible where such a split exists. Hence the absence of a sense of social value is made up for by an exacerbated acceleration of the activities that increase private advantage and power. One cannot look into the inner consciousness of his fellows, but if there is any general degree of inner contentment on the part of those who form our pecuniary oligarchy, the evidence is sadly lacking. As for the many, they are impelled hither and yon by forces beyond their control.

The most marked trait of present life, economically speaking, is insecurity. It is tragic that millions of men desirous of working should be recurrently out of employment; aside from cyclical depressions there is a standing army at all times who have no

regular work. We have not any adequate information as to the
number of these persons. But the ignorance even as to numbers is
slight compared with our inability to grasp the psychological
and moral consequences of the precarious condition in which
vast multitudes live. Insecurity cuts deeper and extends more
widely than bare unemployment. Fear of loss of work, dread of
the oncoming of old age, create anxiety and eat into self-respect
in a way that impairs personal dignity. Where fears abound,
courageous and robust individuality is undermined. The vast
development of technological resources that might bring security
in its train has actually brought a new mode of insecurity, as
mechanization displaces labor. The mergers and consolidations
that mark a corporate age are beginning to bring uncertainty
into the economic lives of the higher salaried class, and that tendency is only just in its early stage. Realization that honest and
industrious pursuit of a calling or business will not guarantee
any stable level of life lessens respect for work and stirs large
numbers to take a chance of some adventitious way of getting
the wealth that will make security possible: witness the orgies of
the stock-market in recent days.

The unrest, impatience, irritation and hurry that are so marked
in American life are inevitable accompaniments of a situation in
which individuals do not find support and contentment in the
fact that they are sustaining and sustained members of a social
whole. They are evidence, psychologically, of abnormality, and it
is as idle to seek for their explanation within the deliberate intent
of individuals as it is futile to think that they can be got rid of by
hortatory moral appeal. Only an acute maladjustment between
individuals and the social conditions under which they live can
account for such widespread pathological phenomena. Feverish
love of anything as long as it is a change which is distracting,
impatience, unsettlement, nervous discontentment, and desire
for excitement, are not native to human nature. They are so
abnormal as to demand explanation in some deep-seated cause.

I should explain a seeming hypocrisy on the same ground. We
are not consciously insincere in our professions of devotion to
ideals of "service"; they mean something. Neither the Rotarian
nor the big business enterprise uses the term merely as a cloak
for "putting something over" which makes for pecuniary gain.
But the lady doth protest too much. The wide currency of such

professions testifies to a sense of a social function of business which is expressed in words because it is so lacking in fact, and yet which is felt to be rightfully there. If our external combinations in industrial activity were reflected in organic integrations of the desires, purposes and satisfactions of individuals, the verbal protestations would disappear, because social utility would be a matter of course.

Some persons hold that a genuine mental counterpart of the outward social scheme is actually forming. Our prevailing mentality, our "ideology," is said to be that of the "business mind" which has become so deplorably pervasive. Are not the prevailing standards of value those derived from pecuniary success and economic prosperity? Were the answer unqualifiedly in the affirmative, we should have to admit that our outer civilization is attaining an inner culture which corresponds to it, however much we might disesteem the quality of that culture. The objection that such a condition is impossible, since man cannot live by bread, by material prosperity alone, is tempting, but it may be said to beg the question. The conclusive answer is that the business mind is not itself unified. It is divided within itself and must remain so as long as the results of industry as the determining force in life are corporate and collective while its animating motives and compensations are so unmitigatedly private. A unified mind, even of the business type, can come into being only when conscious intent and consummation are in harmony with consequences actually effected. This statement expresses conditions so psychologically assured that it may be termed a law of mental integrity. Proof of the existence of the split is found in the fact that while there is much planning of future development with a view to dividends within large business corporations, there is no corresponding coordinated planning of social development.

The growth of corporateness is arbitrarily restricted. Hence it operates to limit individuality, to put burdens on it, to confuse and submerge it. It crowds more out than it incorporates in an ordered and secure life. It has made rural districts stagnant while bringing excess and restless movement to the city. The restriction of corporateness lies in the fact that it remains on the cash level. Men are brought together on the one side by investment in the same joint stock company, and on the other hand by the fact that the machine compels mass production in order that investors may get their profits. The results affect all society in all its phases. But they are as inorganic as the ultimate human motives that operate are private and egoistic. An economic individualism of motives and aims underlies our present corporate mechanisms, and undoes the individual.

The loss of individuality is conspicuous in the economic region because our civilization is so predominantly a business civilization. But the fact is even more obvious when we turn to the political scene. It would be a waste of words to expatiate on the meaninglessness of present political platforms, parties and issues. The old-time slogans are still reiterated, and to a few these words still seem to have a real meaning. But it is too evident to need argument that on the whole our politics, as far as they are not covertly manipulated in behalf of the pecuniary advantage of groups, are in a state of confusion; issues are improvised from week to week with a constant shift of allegiance. It is impossible for individuals to find themselves politically with surety and efficiency under such conditions. Political apathy broken by recurrent sensations and spasms is the natural outcome.

The lack of secure objects of allegiance, without which individuals are lost, is especially striking in the case of the liberal. The liberalism of the past was characterized by the possession of a definite intellectual creed and program; that was its distinction from conservative parties which needed no formulated outlook beyond defense of things as they were. In contrast, liberals operated on the basis of a thought-out social philosophy, a theory of politics sufficiently definite and coherent to be easily translated into a program of policies to be pursued. Liberalism today is hardly more than a temper of mind, vaguely called forward-looking, but quite uncertain as to where to look and what to look forward to. For many individuals, as well as in its social results, this fact is hardly less than a tragedy. The tragedy may be unconscious for the mass, but they show its reality in their aimless drift, while the more thoughtful are consciously disturbed. For human nature is self-possessed only as it has objects to which it can attach itself.

I do not think it is fantastic to connect our excited and rapacious nationalism with the situation in which corporateness has gone so far as to detach individuals from their old local ties and allegiances but not far enough to give them a new centre and order of life. The most militaristic of nations secures the loyalty of its subjects not by physical force but through the power of ideas and emotions. It cultivates ideals of loyalty, of solidarity, and common devotion to a common cause. Modern industry, technology and commerce have created modern nations in their external form. Armies and navies exist to protect commerce, to make secure the control of raw materials, and to command markets. Men would not sacrifice their lives for the purpose of securing economic gain for a few if the conditions presented themselves to their minds in this bald fashion. But the balked demand for genuine cooperativeness and reciprocal solidarity in daily life finds an outlet in nationalistic sentiment. Men have a pathetic instinct toward the adventure of living and struggling together; if the daily community does not feed this impulse, the romantic imagination pictures a grandiose nation in which all are one. If the simple duties of peace do not establish a common life, the emotions are mobilized in the service of a war that will supply its temporary simulation.

I have thus far made no reference to what many persons would consider the most serious and the most overtly evident of all the modes of loss of secure objects of loyalty—religion. It is probably easy to exaggerate the extent of the decadence of religion in an outward sense, church membership, church-going and so on. But it is hardly possible to overstate its decline as a vitally integrative and directive force in men's thought and sentiments. Whether even in the ages of the past that are called religious, religion was itself the actively central force that it is sometimes said to have been may be doubted. But it cannot be doubted that it was the symbol of the existence of conditions and forces that gave unity and a centre to men's views of life. It at least gathered together in weighty and shared symbols a sense of the objects to which men were so attached as to have support and stay in their outlook on life.

Religion does not now effect this result. The divorce of church and state has been followed by that of religion and society. Wherever religion has not become a merely private indulgence, it has become at best a matter of sects and denominations divided from one another by doctrinal differences, and united internally by tenets that have a merely historical origin, and a purely metaphysical or else ritualistic meaning. There is no such bond of social unity as once united Greeks, Romans, Hebrews, and Catholic medieval Europe. There are those who realize what is portended by the loss of religion as an integrating bond. Many of them despair of its recovery through the development of social values to which the imagination and sentiments of individuals can attach themselves with intensity. They wish to reverse the operation and to form the social bond of unity and of allegiance by regeneration of the isolated individual soul.

Aside from the fact that there is no consensus as to what a new religious attitude is to centre itself about, the injunction puts the cart before the horse. Religion is not so much a root of unity as it is its flower or fruit. The very attempt to secure integration for the individual, and through him for society, by means of a deliberate and conscious cultivation of religion, is itself proof of how far the individual has become lost through detachment from acknowledged social values. It is no wonder that when the appeal does not take the form of dogmatic fundamentalism, it tends to terminate in either some form of esoteric occultism or private estheticism. The sense of wholeness which is urged as the essence of religion can be built up and sustained only through membership in a society which has attained a degree of unity. The attempt to cultivate it first in individuals and then extend it to form an organically unified society is fantasy. Indulgence in this fantasy infects such interpretations of American life as are found, to take one signal example, in Waldo Frank's *The Rediscovery of America*.[1] It marks a manner of yearning and not a principle of construction.

For the idea that the outward scene is chaotic because of the machine, which is a principle of chaos, and that it will remain so until individuals reinstitute wholeness within themselves, simply reverses the true state of things. The outward scene, if not fully organized, is relatively so in the corporateness which the machine and its technology have produced; the inner man is the jungle which can be subdued to order only as the forces of organization at work in externals are reflected in corresponding patterns of thought, imagination and emotion. The sick cannot heal themselves by means of their disease, and disintegrated individuals can achieve unity only as the dominant energies of community life are incorporated to form their minds. If these energies were, in reality, mere strivings for private pecuniary gain, the case would indeed be hopeless. But they are constituted by a collective art of technology, which individuals merely deflect to their private ends. There are the beginnings of an objective order through which individuals may get their bearings.

Conspicuous signs of the disintegration of individuality due to failure to reconstruct the self so as to meet the realities of present social life have not been mentioned. In a census that was taken among leaders of opinion concerning the urgency of present social problems, the state of law, the courts, lawlessness and criminality stood at the head of the list, and by a considerable distance. We are even more emphatically than when Kipling wrote the words, the people that make "the laws they flout, and flout the laws they make." We combine an ardor unparalleled in history for "passing" laws with a casual and deliberate disregard for them when they are on the statute books. We believe—to judge by our legislative actions—that we can create morals by law (witness the prohibition amendment for an instance on a large scale) and neglect the fact that all laws except those which regulate technical procedures are registrations of existing social customs and their attendant moral habits and purposes. I can, however, only think of this phenomenon as a symptom, not as a cause. It is a natural expression of a period in which changes in the structure of society have dissolved old bonds and allegiances. We attempt to make good this social relaxation and dissolution by legal enactments, while the actual disintegration discloses itself in the lawlessness which reveals the artificial character of this method of securing social integrity.

Volumes could be formed by collecting articles and editorials written about relaxation of traditional moral codes. A movement has caught public attention, which, having for some obscure reason assumed the name "humanism," proposes restraint and moderation, exercised in and by the higher volition of individuals, as the solution of our ills. It finds that naturalism as practiced by artists and mechanism as taught by philosophers who take their clew from natural science, have broken down the inner laws and imperatives which can alone bring order and loyalty. I should be glad to be able to believe that artists and intellectuals have any such power in their hands; if they had, after using it to bring evil to society, they might change face and bring healing to it. But a sense of fact, together with a sense of humor, forbids the acceptance of any such belief. Literary persons and academic thinkers are now, more than ever, effects, not causes. They reflect and voice the disintegration which new modes of living, produced by new forms of industry and commerce, have introduced. They give witness to the unreality that has overtaken traditional codes in the face of the impact of new forces; indirectly, they proclaim the need of some new synthesis. But this synthesis can be humanistic only as the new conditions are themselves taken into account and are converted into the instrumentalities of a free and humane life. I see no way to "restrain" or turn back the industrial revolution and its consequences. In the absence of such a restraint (which would be efficacious if only it could occur), the urging of some inner restraint through the exercise of the higher personal will, whatever that may be, is itself only a futile echo of just the old individualism that has so completely broken down.

There are many phases of life which illustrate to anyone who chooses to think in terms of realities instead of words the utter irrelevance of the proposed remedy to actual conditions. One might take the present estate of amusements, of the movies, the radio, and organized vicarious sport, and ask just how this powerful eruption in which the resources of technology are employed for economic profit is to be met by the application of the inner *frein* or brake. Perhaps the most striking instance is found in the disintegration due to changes in family life and sex morale. It was not deliberate human intention that undermined the traditional household as the centre of industry and education and as the focus of moral training; that sapped the older institution of enduring marriage. To ask the individuals who suffer the consequences of the general undermining and sapping to put an end to the consequences by acts of personal volition is merely to profess faith in moral magic. Recovery of individuals capable of stable and effective self-control can be had only as there is first a humbler exercise of will to observe existing social realities and to direct them according to their own potentialities.

Instances of the flux in which individuals are loosened from the ties that once gave order and support to their lives are glaring. They are indeed so glaring that they blind our eyes to the causes which produce them. Individuals are groping their way through situations which they do not direct and which do not give them direction. The beliefs and ideals that are uppermost in their consciousness are not relevant to the society in which they outwardly act and which constantly reacts upon them. Their conscious ideas and standards are inherited from an age that has passed away; their minds, as far as consciously entertained principles and methods of interpretation are concerned, are at odds with actual conditions. This profound split is the cause of distraction and bewilderment.

Individuals will refind themselves only as their ideas and ideals are brought into harmony with the realities of the age in which they act. The task of attaining this harmony is not an easy one. But it is more negative than it seems. If we could inhibit the principles and standards that are merely traditional, if we could slough off the opinions that have no living relationship to the situations in which we live, the unavowed forces that now work upon us unconsciously but unremittingly would have a chance to build minds after their own pattern, and individuals might, in consequence, find themselves in possession of objects to which imagination and emotion would stably attach themselves.

I do not mean, however, that the process of rebuilding can go on automatically. Discrimination is required in order to detect the beliefs and institutions that dominate merely because of custom and inertia, and in order to discover the moving realities of the present. Intelligence must distinguish, for example, the tendencies of the technology which produce the new corporateness from those inheritances proceeding out of the individualism of an earlier epoch which arrest and divide the operation of the new dynamics. It is difficult for us to conceive of individualism except in terms of stereotypes derived from former centuries. Individualism has been identified with ideas of initiative and invention that are bound up with private and exclusive economic gain. As long as this conception possesses our minds, the ideal of harmonizing our thought and desire with the realities of present social conditions will be interpreted to mean accommodation and surrender. It will even be understood to signify rationalization of the evils of existing society. A stable recovery of individuality waits upon an elimination of the older economic and political individualism, an elimination which will liberate imagination and endeavor for the task of making corporate society contribute to the free culture of its members. Only by economic revision can the sound element in the older individualism—equality of opportunity—be made a reality.

It is the part of wisdom to note the double meaning of such ideas as "acceptance." There is an acceptance that is of the intellect; it signifies facing facts for what they are. There is another acceptance that is of the emotions and will; that involves commitment of desire and effort. So far are the two from being identical that acceptance in the first sense is the precondition of all intelligent refusal of acceptance in the second sense. There is a prophetic aspect to all observation; we can perceive the meaning of what exists only as we forecast the consequences it entails. When a situation is as confused and divided within itself as is the present social estate, choice is implicated in observation. As one perceives different tendencies and different possible consequences, preference inevitably goes out to one or the other. Because acknowledgment in thought brings with it intelligent discrimination and choice, it is the first step out of confusion, the first step in forming those objects of significant allegiance out of which stable and efficacious individuality may grow. It might even perform the miracle of rendering conservatism relevant and thoughtful. It certainly is the prerequisite of an anchored liberalism.

5. TOWARD A NEW INDIVIDUALISM

Our material culture, as anthropologists would call it, is verging upon the collective and corporate. Our moral culture, along with our ideology, is, on the other hand, still saturated with ideals and values of an individualism derived from the pre-scientific, pre-technological age. Its spiritual roots are found in medieval religion, which asserted the ultimate nature of the individual soul and centered the drama of life about the destiny of that soul. Its institutional and legal concepts were framed in the feudal period.

This moral and philosophical individualism anteceded the rise of modern industry and the era of the machine. It was the context in which the latter operated. The apparent subordination of the individual to established institutions often conceals from recognition the vital existence of a deep-seated individualism. But the fact that the controlling institution was the Church should remind us that in ultimate intent it existed to secure the salvation of the individual. That this individual was conceived as a soul, and that the end served by the institution was deferred to another and everlasting life conceal from contemporary realization the underlying individualism. In its own time, its substance consisted in just this eternal spiritual character of the personal soul; the power of the established institutions proceeded from their being the necessary means of accomplishing the supreme end of the individual.

The early phase of the industrial revolution wrought a great transformation. It gave a secular and worldly turn to the career of the individual, and it liquefied the static property concepts of feudalism by the shift of emphasis from agriculture to manufacturing. Still, the idea persisted that property and reward were intrinsically individual. There were, it is true, incompatible elements in the earlier and later versions of individualism. But a fusion of individual capitalism, of natural rights, and of morals founded in strictly individual traits and values remained, under the influence of Protestantism, the dominant intellectual synthesis.

The basis of this synthesis was destroyed, however, by the later development of the industrial system, which brought about the merging of personal capacity, effort and work into collective wholes. Meanwhile, the control of natural energies eliminated time and distance, so that action once adapted to local conditions was swallowed up in complex undertakings of indefinite extent. Yet the older mental equipment remained after its causes and foundations had disappeared. This, fundamentally, is the inner division out of which spring our present confusion and insincerities.

The earlier economic individualism had a definite creed and function. It sought to release from legal restrictions man's wants and his efforts to satisfy those wants. It believed that such emancipation would stimulate latent energy into action, would automatically assign individual ability to the work for which it was suited, would cause it to perform that work under stimulus of the advantage to be gained, and would secure for capacity and enterprise the reward and position to which they were entitled. At the same time, individual energy and savings would be serving the needs of others, and thus promoting the general welfare and effecting a general harmony of interests.

We have gone a long way since this philosophy was formulated. Today, the most stalwart defenders of this type of individualism do not venture to repeat its optimistic assertions. At most, they are content to proclaim its consistency with unchanging human nature—which is said to be moved to effort only by the hope of personal gain—and to paint dire pictures of the inevitable consequences of change to any other regime. They ascribe all the material benefits of our present civilization to this individualism—as if machines were made by the desire for money profit, not by impersonal science; and as if they were driven by money alone, and not by electricity and steam under the direction of a collective technology.

In America, the older individualism assumed a romantic form. It was hardly necessary to elaborate a theory which equated personal gain with social advance. The demands of the practical situation called for the initiative, enterprise and vigor of individuals in all immediate work that urgently asked for doing, and their operation furthered the national life. The spirit of the time is expressed by Dr. Crothers, whose words Mr. Sims has appropriately taken for part of the text of his "Adventurous America":

> If you would understand the driving power of America,
> you must understand "the divers discontented and impatient
> young men" who in each generation have found an outlet for
> their energy. . . . The noises which disturb you are not the
> cries of an angry proletariat, but are the shouts of eager
> young people who are finding new opportunities. . . . They
> represent today the enthusiasm of a new generation. They
> represent the Oregons and Californias toward which sturdy
> pioneers are moving undisturbed by obstacles. This is what
> the social unrest means in America.

If that is not an echo of the echo of a voice of long ago, I do not know what it is. I do not, indeed, hear the noises of an angry proletariat; but I should suppose the sounds heard are the murmurs of lost opportunities, along with the din of machinery, motor cars and speakeasies, by which the murmurs of discontent are drowned, rather than shouts of eagerness for adventurous opportunity.

The European version of the older individualism had its value and temporal justification because the new technology needed liberation from vexatious legal restrictions. Machine industry was itself in a pioneer condition, and those who carried it forward against obstacles of lethargy, skepticism and political obstruction were deserving of special reward. Moreover, accumulation of capital was thought of in terms of enterprises that today would be petty; there was no dream of the time when it would reach such a mass that it would determine the legal and political order. Poverty had previously been accepted as a dispensation of nature that was inevitable. The new industry promised a way out, at least to those possessed of energy and will to save and accumulate. But there was no anticipation of a time when the development of machine technology would afford the material basis for reasonable ease and comfort and of extensive leisure for all.

The shift that makes the older individualism a dying echo is more marked as well as more rapid in this country. Where is the wilderness which now beckons creative energy and affords untold opportunity to initiative and vigor? Where is the pioneer who goes forth rejoicing, even in the midst of privation, to its conquest? The wilderness exists in the movie and the novel, and the children of the pioneers, who live in the midst of surroundings artificially made over by the machine, enjoy pioneer life idly in the vicarious film. I see little social unrest which is the straining of energy for outlet in action; I find rather the protest against a weakening of vigor and a sapping of energy that emanate from the absence of constructive opportunity; and I see a confusion that is an expression of the inability to find a secure and morally rewarding place in a troubled and tangled economic scene.

Because of the bankruptcy of the older individualism, those who are aware of the break-down often speak and argue as if individualism were itself done and over with. I do not suppose that those who regard socialism and individualism as antithetical really mean that individuality is going to die out or that it is not something intrinsically precious. But in speaking as if the only individualism were the local episode of the last two centuries, they play into the hands of those who would keep it alive in order to serve their own ends, and they slur over the chief problem—that of remaking society to serve the growth of a new type of individual. There are many who believe that socialism of some form is needed to realize individual initiative and security on a wide scale. They are concerned about the restriction of power and freedom to a few in the present regime, and they think that collective social control is necessary, at least for a time, in order to achieve its advantages for all. But they too often seem to assume that the result will be merely an extension of the earlier individualism to the many.

Such thinking treats individualism as if it were something static, having a uniform content. It ignores the fact that the mental and moral structure of individuals, the pattern of their desires and purposes, change with every great change in social constitution. Individuals who are not bound together in associations, whether domestic, economic, religious, political, artistic or educational, are monstrosities. It is absurd to suppose that the ties which hold them together are merely external and do not react into mentality and character, producing the framework of personal disposition.

The tragedy of the "lost individual" is due to the fact that while individuals are now caught up into a vast complex of associations, there is no harmonious and coherent reflection of the import of these connections into the imaginative and emotional outlook on life. This fact is of course due in turn to the absence of harmony within the state of society. There is an undoubted circle. But it is a vicious circle only as far as men decline to accept—in the intellectual, observing and inquiring spirit defined in the previous chapter—the realities of the social estate, and because of this refusal either surrender to the division or seek to save their individuality by escape or sheer emotional revolt. The habit of opposing the corporate and collective to the individual tends to the persistent continuation of the confusion and uncertainty. It distracts attention from the crucial issue: How shall the individual refind himself in an unprecedentedly new social situation, and what qualities will the new individualism exhibit?

That the problem is not merely one of extending to all individuals the traits of economic initiative, opportunity and enterprise; that it is one of forming a new psychological and moral type, is suggested by the great pressure now brought to bear to effect conformity and standardization of American opinion. Why should regimentation, the erection of an average struck from the opinions of large masses into regulative norms, and in general the domination of quantity over quality, be so characteristic of present American life? I see but one fundamental explanation. The individual cannot remain intellectually a vacuum. If his ideas and beliefs are not the spontaneous function of a communal life in which he shares, a seeming consensus will be secured as a substitute by artificial and mechanical means. In the absence of mentality that is congruous with the new social corporateness that is coming into being, there is a desperate effort to fill the void by external agencies which obtain a factitious agreement.

In consequence, our uniformity of thought is much more superficial than it seems to be. The standardization is deplorable, but one might almost say that one of the reasons it is deplorable is because it does not go deep. It goes far enough to effect suppression of original quality of thought, but not far enough to achieve enduring unity. Its superficial character is evident in its instability. All agreement of thought obtained by external means, by repression and intimidation, however subtle, and by calculated propaganda and publicity, is of necessity superficial; and whatever is superficial is in continual flux. The methods employed produce mass credulity, and this jumps from one thing to another according to the dominant suggestions of the day. We think and feel alike—but only for a month or a season. Then comes some other sensational event or personage to exercise a hypnotizing uniformity of response. At a given time, taken in cross-section, conformity is the rule. In a time span, taken longitudinally, instability and flux dominate. . . . I suppose there are others who have a feeling of irritation at such terms as "radio-conscious" and "air-minded," now so frequently forced upon us. I do not think the irritation is wholly due to linguistic causes. It testifies to a half-conscious sense of the external ways in which our minds are formed and swayed and of the superficiality and inconsistency of the result.

There are, I suppose, those who fancy that the emphasis which I put upon the corporateness of existing society in the United States is in effect, even if not in the writer's conscious intent, a plea for greater conformity than now exists. Nothing could be further from the truth. Identification of society with a level, whatever it be, high as well as low, of uniformity is just another evidence of that distraction because of which the individual is lost. Society is of course but the relations of individuals to one another in this form and that. And all relations are interactions, not fixed molds. The particular interactions that compose a human society include the give and take of participation, of a sharing that increases, that expands and deepens, the capacity and significance of the interacting factors. Conformity is a name for the absence of vital interplay; the arrest and benumbing of communication. As I have been trying to say, it is the artificial substitute used to hold men together in lack of associations that are incorporated into inner dispositions of thought and desire. I often wonder what meaning is given to the term "society" by those who oppose it to the intimacies of personal intercourse, such as those of friendship. Presumably they have in their minds a picture of rigid institutions or some set and external organization. But an institution that is other than the structure of human contact and intercourse is a fossil of some past society; organization, as in any living organism, is the cooperative consensus of multitudes of cells, each living in exchange with others.

I should suppose that the more intelligent of those who wield the publicity agencies which produce conformity would be disturbed at beholding their own success. I can easily understand that they should have a cynical sense of their ability to obtain the results they want at a given time; but I should think they would fear that like-mindedness might, at a critical juncture, veer in an unexpected direction and turn with equal unanimity against the things and interests it has been manipulated to support. Crowd psychology is dangerous in its instability. To rely upon it for permanent support is playing with a fire that may get out of control. Conformity is enduringly effective when it is a spontaneous and largely unconscious manifestation of the agreements that spring from genuine communal life. An artificially induced uniformity of thought and sentiment is a symptom of an inner void. Not all of it that now exists is intentionally produced; it is not the result of deliberate manipulation. But it is, on the other hand, the result of causes so external as to be accidental and precarious.

The "joining" habit of the average American, and his excessive sociability, may well have an explanation like that of conformity. They, too, testify to nature's abhorrence of that vacuum which the passing of the older individualism has produced. We should not be so averse to solitude if we had, when we were alone, the companionship of communal thought built into our mental habits. In the absence of this communion, there is the need for reinforcement by external contact. Our sociability is largely an effort to find substitutes for that normal consciousness of connection and union that proceeds from being a sustained and sustaining member of a social whole.

Just as the new individualism cannot be achieved by extending the benefits of the older economic individualism to more persons, so it cannot be obtained by a further development of generosity, good will and altruism. Such traits are desirable, but they are also more or less constant expressions of human nature. There is much in the present situation that stimulates them to active operation. They are probably more marked features of American life than of that of any other civilization at any time.

Our charity and philanthropy are partly the manifestation of an uneasy conscience. As such a manifestation, they testify to a realization that a régime of industry carried on for private gain does not satisfy the full human nature of even those who profit by it. The impulse and need which the existing economic régime chokes, through preventing its articulated expression, find outlet in actions that acknowledge a social responsibility which the system as a system denies. Hence the development of philanthropic measures is not only compensatory to a stifling of human nature undergone in business, but it is in a way prophetic. Construction is better than relief; prevention than cure. Activities by way of relief of poverty and its attendant mental strains and physical ills—and our philanthropic activities including even the endowment of educational institutions have their ultimate causes in the existence of economic insecurity and distress—suggest, in dim forecast, a society in which daily occupations and relationships will give independence and substantial living to all normal individuals who share in its ongoings, reserving relief for extraordinary emergencies. One does not need to reflect upon the personal motives of great philanthropists to see in what they do an emphatic record of the breakdown of our existing economic organization.

For the chief obstacle to the creation of a type of individual whose pattern of thought and desire is enduringly marked by consensus with others, and in whom sociability is one with co-operation in all regular human associations, is the persistence of that feature of the earlier individualism which defines industry and commerce by ideas of private pecuniary profit. Why, once more, is there such zeal for standardized likeness? It is not, I imagine, because conformity for its own sake appears to be a great boon. It is rather because a certain kind of conformity gives defense and protection to the pecuniary features of our present regime. The foreground may be filled with depiction of the horror of change, and with clamor for law and order and the support of the Constitution. But behind there is desire for perpetuation of that regime which defines individual initiative and ability by success in conducting business so as to make money.

It is not too much to say that the whole significance of the older individualism has now shrunk to a pecuniary scale and measure. The virtues that are supposed to attend rugged individualism may be vocally proclaimed, but it takes no great insight to see that what is cherished is measured by its connection with those activities that make for success in business conducted for personal gain. Hence, the irony of the gospel of "individualism" in business conjoined with suppression of individuality in thought and speech. One cannot imagine a bitterer comment on any professed individualism than that it subordinates the only creative individuality—that of mind—to the maintenance of a regime which gives the few an opportunity for being shrewd in the management of monetary business.

It is claimed, of course, that the individualism of economic self-seeking, even if it has not produced the adjustment of ability and reward and the harmony of interests earlier predicted, has given us the advantage of material prosperity. It is not needful to raise here the question of how far that material prosperity extends. For it is not true that its moving cause is pecuniary individualism. That has been the cause of some great fortunes, but not of national wealth; it counts in the process of distribution, but not in ultimate creation. Scientific insight taking effect in machine technology has been the great productive force. For the most part, economic individualism interpreted as energy and enterprise devoted to private profit, has been an adjunct, often a parasitical one, to the movement of technical and scientific forces.

The scene in which individuality is created has been transformed. The pioneer, such as is depicted in the quotation from Crothers, had no great need for any ideas beyond those that sprang up in the immediate tasks in which he was engaged. His intellectual problems grew out of struggle with the forces of physical nature. The wilderness was a reality and it had to be subdued. The type of character that evolved was strong and hardy, often picturesque, and sometimes heroic. Individuality was a reality because it corresponded to conditions. Irrelevant traditional ideas in religion and morals were carried along, but they were reduced to a size where they did no harm; indeed, they could easily be interpreted in such a way as to be a reinforcement to the sturdy and a consolation to the weak and failing.

But it is no longer a physical wilderness that has to be wrestled with. Our problems grow out of social conditions: they concern human relations rather than man's direct relationship to physical nature. The adventure of the individual, if there is to be any venturing of individuality and not a relapse into the deadness of complacency or of despairing discontent, is an unsubdued social frontier. The issues cannot be met with ideas improvised for the occasion. The problems to be solved are general, not local. They concern complex forces that are at work throughout the whole country, not those limited to an immediate and almost face-to-face environment. Traditional ideas are more than irrelevant. They are an encumbrance; they are the chief obstacle to the formation of a new individuality integrated within itself and with a liberated function in the society wherein it exists. A new individualism can be achieved only through the controlled use of all the resources of the science and technology that have mastered the physical forces of nature.

They are not controlled now in any fundamental sense. Rather do they control us. They are indeed physically controlled. Every factory, power-house and railway system testifies to the fact that we have attained this measure of control. But control of power through the machine is not control of the machine itself. Control of the energies of nature by science is not controlled use of science. We are not even approaching a climax of control; we are hardly at its feeble beginnings. For control is relative to consequences, ends, values; and we do not manage, we hardly have commenced to dream of managing, physical power for the sake of projected purposes and prospective goods. The machine took us unawares and unprepared. Instead of forming new purposes commensurate with its potentialities, we accordingly tried to make it the servant of aims that were the expression of an age when mastery of natural energies on any large scale was the fantasy of magic. As Clarence Ayres has said: "Our industrial revolution began, as some historians say, with half a dozen technical improvements in the textile industry; and it took us a century to realize that anything of moment had happened to us beyond the obvious improvement of spinning and weaving."

I do not say that the aims and values of the earlier day were petty in themselves. But they are almost inconceivably petty in comparison with the means now at our command—if we had an imagination large enough to encompass their potential uses. They are worse than petty; they are confusing and distracting when men are confronted with the physical instrumentalities and agencies which, in the lack of comprehensive purpose and concerted planning, work blindly and carry us drifting hither and yon. I cannot obtain intellectual, moral or esthetic satisfaction from the professed philosophy which animates Bolshevik Russia. But I am sure that the future historian of our times will combine admiration of those who had the imagination first to see that the resources of technology might be directed by organized planning to serve chosen ends with astonishment at the intellectual and moral hebetude of other peoples who were technically so much further advanced.

There is no greater sign of the paralysis of the imagination which custom and involvement in immediate detail can induce than the belief, sedulously propagated by some who pride themselves on superior taste, that the machine is itself the source of our troubles. Of course immense potential resources impose responsibility, and it has yet to be demonstrated whether human capacity can rise to utilization of the opportunities which the machine and technology have opened to us. But it is hard to think of anything more childish than the animism that puts the blame on machinery. For machinery means an undreamed-of reservoir of power. If we have harnessed this power to the dollar rather than to the liberation and enrichment of human life, it is because we have been content to stay within the bounds of traditional aims and values although we are in possession of a revolutionary transforming instrument. Repetition of the older credo of individualism is but the evidence of contentment within these bonds. I for one think it is incredible that this particular form of confession of inferiority will endure very much longer. When we begin to ask what can be done with the machine for the creation and fulfillment of values corresponding to its potency and begin organized planning to effect these goods, a new individual correlative to the realities of the age in which we live will also begin to take form.

Revolt against the machine as the author of social evils usually has an esthetic origin. A more intellectual and quasi-philosophic reaction finds natural science to be their source; or if not science itself (which is allowed to be all very well if it keeps its appropriate humble place) then the attitude of those who depend upon science as an organ of vision and light. Contempt for nature is understandable, at least historically; even though it seems both intellectually petty and morally ungracious to feel contempt for the matrix of our being and the inescapable condition of our lives. But that men should fear and dislike the method of approach to nature I do not find understandable. The eye sees many foul things and the arm and hand do many cruel things. Yet the fanatic who would pluck out the eye and cut off the arm is recognized for what he is. Science, one may say, is but the extension of our natural organs of approach to nature. And I do not mean merely an extension in quantitative range and penetration, as a microscope multiplies the capacity of the unaided eye, but an extension of insight and understanding through bringing relationships and interactions into view. Since we must in any case approach nature in some fashion and by some path—if only that of death—I confess my total inability to understand those who object to an intelligently controlled approach—for that is what science is.

The only way in which I can obtain any sympathetic realization of their attitude is by recalling that there have been those who have professed adoration of science—writing it with a capital S—; those who have thought of it not as a method of approach but as a kind of self-enclosed entity and end in itself, a new theology of self-sufficient authoritatively revealed inherent and absolute Truth. It would, however, seem simpler to correct their misapprehension than first to share it and then to reverse their worship into condemnation. The opposite of intelligent method is no method at all or blind and stupid method. It is a curious state of mind which finds pleasure in setting forth the "limits of science." For the intrinsic limit of knowledge is simply ignorance; and the point in extolling ignorance is not clear except when expressed by those who profit by keeping others in ignorance. There is of course an extrinsic limit of science. But that limitation lies in the ineptitude of those who put it to use; its removal lies in rectification of its use, not in abuse of the thing used.

This reference to science and technology is relevant because they are the forces of present life which are finally significant. It is through employing them with understanding of their possible import that a new individualism, consonant with the realities of the present age, may be brought into operative being. There are many levels and many elements in both the individual and his relations. Neither can be comprehended nor dealt with in mass. Discriminative sensitivity, selection, is imperative. Art is the fruit of such selection when it is given objective effect. The art which our times needs in order to create a new type of individuality is the art which, being sensitive to the technology and science that are the moving forces of our time, will envisage the expansive, the social, culture which they may be made to serve. I am not anxious to depict the form which this emergent individualism will assume. Indeed, I do not see how it can be described until more progress has been made in its production. But such progress will not be initiated until we cease opposing the socially corporate to the individual, and until we develop a constructively imaginative observation of the role of science and technology in actual society. The greatest obstacle to that vision is, I repeat, the perpetuation of the older individualism now reduced, as I have said, to the utilization of science and technology for ends of private pecuniary gain. I sometimes wonder if those who are conscious of present ills but who direct their blows of criticism at everything except this obstacle are not stirred by motives which they unconsciously prefer to keep below consciousness.

6. CAPITALISM OR PUBLIC SOCIALISM

I once heard a distinguished lawyer say that the earlier American ideas about individual initiative and enterprise could be recovered by an amendment of a few lines to the federal Constitution. The amendment would prohibit all joint stock enterprises and permit only individual liability to have a legal status. He was, I think, the only unadulterated Jeffersonian Democrat I have ever met. He was also logical. He did not delude himself into supposing that the pioneer gospel of personal initiative, enterprise, energy and reward could be maintained in an era of aggregated corporate capital, of mass production and distribution, of impersonal ownership and of ownership divorced from management. Our political life, however, continues to ignore the change that has taken place except as circumstances force it to take account of it in sporadic matters.

The myth is still current that socialism desires to use political means in order to divide wealth equally among all individuals, and that it is consequently opposed to the development of trusts, mergers and consolidated business in general. It is regarded, in other words, as a kind of arithmetically fractionized individualism. This notion of socialism is of the sort that would naturally be entertained by those who cannot get away from the inherent conception of the individual as an isolated and independent unit. In reality, Karl Marx was the prophet of just this period of economic consolidation. If his ghost hovers above the American scene, it must find legitimate satisfaction in our fulfilment of his predictions.

In these predictions, however, Marx reasoned too much from psychological economic premises and depended too little upon technological causes—the application of science to steam, electricity and chemical processes. That is to say, he argued to an undue extent from an alleged constant appropriation by capitalists of all surplus values created by the workers—surplus being defined as anything above the minimum needed for their continued subsistence. He had no conception, moreover, of the capacity of expanding industry to develop new inventions so as to develop new wants, new forms of wealth, new occupations; nor did ne imagine that the intellectual ability of the employing class would be equal to seeing the need for sustaining consuming power by high wages in order to keep up production and its profits. This explains why his prediction of a revolution in political control, caused by the general misery of the masses and resulting in the establishment of a socialistic society, has not been realized in this country. Nevertheless, the issue which he raised—the relation of the economic structure to political operations—is one that actively persists.

Indeed, it forms the only basis of present political questions. An intelligent and experienced observer of affairs at Washington has said that all political questions which he has heard discussed in Washington come back ultimately to problems connected with the distribution of income. Wealth, property and the processes of manufacturing and distribution—down to retail trade through the chain system—can hardly be socialized in outward effect without a political repercussion. It constitutes an ultimate issue which must be faced by new or existing political parties. There is still enough vitality in the older individualism to offer a very serious handicap to any party or program which calls itself by the name of Socialism. But in the long run, the realities of the situation will exercise control over the connotations which, for historical reasons, cling to a word. In view of this fact, the fortunes of a party called by a given name are insignificant.

In one important sense, the fundamental character of the economic question is not ignored in present politics. The dominant party has officially constituted itself the guardian of prosperity; it has gone further and offered itself as the author of prosperity. It has insinuated itself in that guise into the imagination of a sufficient number of citizens and voters so that it owes its continuing domination to its identification with prosperity. Our presidential elections are upon the whole determined by fear. Hundreds of thousands of citizens who vote independently or for Democratic candidates at local elections and in off-year congressional elections regularly vote the Republican ticket every four years. They do so because of a vague but influential dread lest a monkey-wrench be thrown into the economic and financial machine. The dread is as general among the workers as among small traders and storekeepers. It is basically the asset that keeps the dominant party in office. Our whole industrial scheme is so complex, so delicately interdependent in its varied parts, so responsive to a multitude of subtle influences, that it seems definitely better to the mass of voters to endure the ills they may already suffer rather than take the chance of disturbing industry. Even in the election of 1928, in spite of both the liquor and the Catholic issue, this was, I believe, the determining factor.

Moreover, the fact that Hoover offered himself to the popular imagination as a man possessed of the engineer's rather than the politician's mind was a great force. Engineering has accomplished great things; its triumphs are everywhere in evidence. The miracles that it has wrought have given it the prestige of magical wonder-working. A people sick of politicians felt in some half-conscious way that the mind, experience and gifts of an engineer would bring healing and order into our political life. It is impossible to present statistics as to the exact force of the factors mentioned. Judgment on the two points, especially the latter, must remain a matter of opinion. But the identification of the Republican party with the maintenance of prosperity cannot be denied, and the desire for the engineer in politics is general enough to be at least symptomatic.

Prosperity is largely a state of mind, and belief in it is even more so. It follows that skepticism about its extent is of little importance when the mental tide runs with the idea. Although figures can be quoted to show how spotty it is, and how inequitably its economic conditions are distributed, they are all to no avail. What difference does it make that eleven thousand people, having each an annual income of over $100,000, appropriated in 1927 about one twenty-fifth of the net national income? What good does it do to cite official figures showing that only 20 percent of the income of the favored eleven thousand came from salaries and from profits of the businesses they were personally engaged in, while the remaining 80 percent was derived from investments, speculative profits, rent, etc.? That the total earnings of eight million wage workers should be only four times the amount of what the income-tax returns frankly call the "unearned" income of the eleven thousand millionaires goes almost without notice. Moreover, income from investments in corporate aggregations increases at the expense of that coming from enterprises personally managed. For anyone to call attention to this discrepancy is considered an aspersion on our rugged individualism and an attempt to stir up class feeling. Meanwhile, the income-tax returns for 1928 show that in seven years the number of persons having an annual income of more than $1,000,000 has increased from sixty-seven to almost five hundred, twenty-four of whom had incomes of over $10,000,000 each.

Nevertheless, the assumption of guardianship of prosperity by a political party means the assumption of responsibility, and in the long run the ruling economic-political combination will be held to account. The over-lords will have to do something to make good. This fact seems to me to be the centre of the future political situation. Discussion of the prospective political development in connection with corporate industry may at least start from the fact that the industries which used to be regarded as staple, as the foundations of sound economy, are depressed. The plight of agriculture, of the coal and textile industries, is well known. The era of great railway expansion has come to a close; the building trades have a fluctuating career. The counterpart of this fact is that the now flourishing industries are those connected with and derived from new technical developments. Without the rapid growth in the manufacture and sale of automobiles, radios, airplanes, etc.; without the rapid development of new uses for electricity and super-power, prosperity in the last few years would hardly have been even a state of mind. Economic stimulus has come largely from these new uses for capital and labor; surplus funds drawn from them have kept the stock market and other forms of business actively going. At the same time, these newer developments have accelerated the accumulation and concentration of super-fortunes.

These facts seem to suggest the issue of future politics. The fact of depression has already influenced political action in legislation and administration. What will happen when industries now new become in turn overcapitalized and consumption does not keep up in proportion to investment in them; when they, too, have an excess capacity of production? There are now, it is estimated, eight billions of surplus savings a year, and the amount is increasing. Where is this capital to find its outlet? Diversion into the stock market gives temporary relief, but the resulting inflation is a "cure" which creates a new disease. If it goes into the expansion of industrial plants, how long will it be before they, too, "overproduce"? The future seems to hold in store an extension of political control in the social interest. We already have the Interstate Commerce Commission, the Federal Reserve Board, and now the Farm Relief Board—a socialistic undertaking on a large scale sponsored by the party of individualism. The probabilities seem to favor the creation of more such boards in the future, in spite of all concomitant denunciations of bureaucracy and proclamations that individualism is the source of our national prosperity.

The tariff question, too, is undergoing a change. Now, it is the older industries which, being depressed, clamor for relief. The "infant" industries are those which are indifferent, and which, with their growing interest in export trade, are likely to become increasingly indifferent or hostile. The alignment of political parties has not indeed been affected so far by economic changes— beyond the formation of insurgent blocs within the old parties. But this fact only conceals from view the greater fact that, under cover of the old parties, legislation and administration have taken on new functions due to the impact of trade and finance. The most striking example, of course, is the effort to use governmental agencies and large public funds to put agriculture on a parity with other forms of industry. The case is the more significant because the farmers form the part of the population that has remained most faithful to the old individualistic philosophy, and because the movement is definitely directed to bringing them within the scope of collective and corporate action. The policy of using public works to alleviate unemployment in times of depression is another, if lesser, sign of the direction which political action is taking.

The question of whether and how far the newer industries will follow the cycle of the older and now depressed ones, becoming overcapitalized, overproductive in capacity and overcharged with carrying costs, is, of course, a speculative one. The negative side of the argument demands, however, considerable optimism. It is at least reasonably certain that if depression sets in with them, the process of public intervention and public control will be repeated. And in any case, nothing can permanently exclude political action with reference to old age and unemployment. The scandalous absence even of public inquiry and statistics is emphasized at present by the displacement of workers through technical developments, and by the lowering, because of speeded-up processes, of the age-limit at which workers can be profitably employed. Unemployment, on the scale at which it now "normally" exists—to say nothing of its extent during cyclic periods of depression—is a confession of the breakdown of unregulated individualistic industry conducted for private profit. Coal miners and even farmers may go unheeded, but not so the industrial city workers. One of the first signs of the reawakening of an aggressive labor movement will be the raising of the unemployment problem to a political issue. The outcome of this will be a further extension of public control.

Political prophecy is a risky affair and I would not venture into details. But large and basic economic currents cannot be ignored for any great length of time, and they are working in one direction. There are many indications that the reactionary tendencies which have controlled American politics are coming to a term. The inequitable distribution of income will bring to the fore the use of taxing power to effect redistribution by means of larger taxation of swollen income and by heavier death duties on large fortunes. The scandal of private appropriation of socially produced values in unused land cannot forever remain unconcealed. The situation in world production and commerce is giving "protection and free trade" totally new meanings. The connection of municipal mismanagement and corruption with special favors to big economic interests, and the connection of the alliance thus formed with crime, are becoming more generally recognized. Local labor bodies are getting more and more discontented with the policy of political abstention and with the farce of working through parties controlled by adverse interests. The movement is cumulative and includes convergence to a common head of many now isolated factors. When a focus is reached, economic issues will be openly and not merely covertly political. The problem of social control of industry and the use of governmental agencies for constructive social ends will become the avowed centre of political struggle.

A chapter is devoted to the political phase of the situation not because it is supposed the place of definitely political action in the resolution of the present split in life is fundamental. But it is accessory. A certain amount of specific change in legislation and administration is required in order to supply the conditions under which other changes may take place in non-political ways. Moreover, the psychological effect of law and political discussion is enormous. Political action provides large-scale models that react into the formation of ideas and ideals about all social matters. One sure way in which the individual who is politically lost, because of the loss of objects to which his loyalties can attach themselves, could recover a composed mind, would be by apprehension of the realities of industry and finance as they function in public and political life. Political apathy such as has marked our thought for many years past is due fundamentally to mental confusion arising from lack of consciousness of any vital connection between politics and daily affairs. The parties have been eager accomplices in maintaining the confusion and unreality. To know where things are going and why they are is to have the material out of which stable objects of purpose and loyalty may be formed. To perceive clearly the actual movement of events is to be on the road to intellectual clarity and order.

The chief value of political reference is that politics so well exemplify the existing social confusion and its causes. The various expressions of public control to which reference has been made have taken place sporadically and in response to the pressure of distressed groups so large that their voting power demanded attention. They have been improvised to meet special occasions. They have not been adopted as parts of any general social policy. Consequently their real import has not been considered; they have been treated as episodic exceptions. We live politically from hand to mouth. Corporate forces are strong enough to secure attention and action now and then, when some emergency forces them upon us, but acknowledgment of them does not inspire consecutive policy. On the other hand, the older individualism is still sufficiently ingrained to obtain allegiance in confused sentiment and in vocal utterance. It persists to such an extent that we can maintain the illusion that it regulates our political thought and behavior. In actuality, appeal to it serves to perpetuate the current disorganization in which financial and industrial power, corporately organized, can deflect economic consequences away from the advantage of the many to serve the privilege of the few.

I know of no recent event so politically interesting as President Hoover's calling of industrial conferences after the stock-market crash of 1929. It is indicative of many things, some of them actual, some of them dimly and ambiguously possible. It testifies to the disturbance created when the prospect of an industrial depression faces a party and administration that have assumed responsibility for prosperity through having claimed credit for it. It testifies to the import of the crowd psychology of suggestion and credulity in American life. Christian Science rules American thought in business affairs; if we can be led to think that certain things do not exist, they perforce have not happened. These conferences also give evidence of our national habit of planlessness in social affairs, of locking the barn-door after the horse has been stolen. For nothing was done until after a crash which every economist—except those hopelessly committed to the doctrine of a "new economic era"—knew was certain to happen, however uncertain they may have been as to its time.

The more ambiguous meaning of these conferences is connected with future developments. It is clear that one of their functions was to add up columns of figures to imposing totals, with a view to their effect on the public imagination. Will there be more than a psychological and arithmetical outcome? A hopeful soul may take it as the beginning of a real application of the engineering mind to social life in its economic phase. He may persuade himself that it is the commencement of the acceptance of social responsibility on a large scale by American industrialists, financiers and politicians. He may envisage a permanent Economic Council finally growing out of the holding of a series of conferences, a council which shall take upon itself a planned coordination of industrial development. He may be optimistic enough to anticipate a time when representatives of labor will meet on equal terms, not for the sake of obtaining a pledge to abstain from efforts to obtain a rise of wages and from strikes, but as an integral factor in maintaining a planned regulation of the bases of national welfare.

The issue is still in the future and uncertain. What is not uncertain is that any such move would, if carried through, mark the acknowledged end of the old social and political epoch and its dominant philosophy. It would be in accord with the spirit of American life if the movement were undertaken by voluntary agreement and endeavor rather than by governmental coercion. There is that much enduring truth in our individualism. But the outcome would surely involve the introduction of social responsibility into our business system to such an extent that the doom of an exclusively pecuniary-profit industry would follow. A coordinating and directive council in which captains of industry and finance would meet with representatives of labor and public officials to plan the regulation of industrial activity would signify that we had entered constructively and voluntarily upon the road which Soviet Russia is traveling with so much attendant destruction and coercion. While, as I have already said, political action is not basic, concentration of attention upon real and vital issues such as attend the public control of industry and finance for the sake of social values would have vast intellectual and emotional reverberations. No phase of our culture would remain unaffected. Politics is a means, not an end. But thought of it as a means will lead to thought of the ends it should serve. It will induce consideration of the ways in which a worthy and rich life for all may be achieved. In so doing, it will restore directive aims and be a significant step forward in the recovery of a unified individuality.

I have tried to make a brief survey of the possibilities of the political situation in general, and not to make either a plea or a prophecy of special political alignments. But any kind of political regeneration within or without the present parties demands first of all a frank intellectual recognition of present tendencies. In a society so rapidly becoming corporate, there is need of associated thought to take account of the realities of the situation and to frame policies in the social interest. Only then can organized action in behalf of the social interest be made a reality. We are in for some kind of socialism, call it by whatever name we please, and no matter what it will be called when it is realized. Economic determinism is now a fact, not a theory. But there is a difference and a choice between a blind, chaotic and unplanned determinism, issuing from business conducted for pecuniary profit, and the determination of a socially planned and ordered development. It is the difference and the choice between a socialism that is public and one that is capitalistic.

7. THE CRISIS IN CULTURE

Discussion of the state and prospects of American culture abounds. But "culture" is an ambiguous word. With respect to one of its meanings I see no ground for pessimism. Interest in art, science and philosophy is not on the wane; the contrary is the case. There may have been individuals superior in achievement in the past, but I do not know of any time in our history when so many persons were actively concerned, both as producers and as appreciators, with these culminating aspects of civilization. There is a more lively and more widespread interest in ideas, in critical discussion, in all that forms an intellectual life, than ever before. Anyone who can look back over a span of thirty or forty years must be conscious of the difference that a generation has produced. And the movement is going forward, not backward.

About culture in the sense of cultivation of a number of persons, a number on the increase rather than the decrease, I find no ground for any great solicitude. But "culture" has another meaning. It denotes the type of emotion and thought that is characteristic of a people and epoch as a whole, an organic intellectual and moral quality. Without raising the ambiguous question of aristocracy, one can say without fear of denial that a high degree of personal cultivation at the top of society can coexist with a low and unworthy state of culture as a pervasive manifestation of social life. The marvelous achievement of the novel, music and the drama in the Russia of the Tsar's day sufficiently illustrates what is meant. Nor is preoccupation with commerce and wealth an insuperable bar to a flourishing culture. One may cite the fact that the highest phase of Dutch painting came in a time of just such expansion. And so it was with the Periclean, Augustan and Elizabethan ages. Excellence of personal cultivation has often, and perhaps usually, been coincident with the political and economic dominance of a few and with periods of material expansion.

I see no reason why we in the United States should not also have golden ages of literature and science. But we are given to looking at this and that "age" marked with great names and great productivity, while forgetting to ask about the roots of the efflorescence. Might it not be argued that the very transitoriness of the glory of these ages proves that its causes were sporadic and accidental? And in any case, a question must be raised as to the growth of native culture in our own country. The idea of democracy is doubtless as ambiguous as is that of aristocracy. But we cannot evade a basic issue. Unless an avowedly democratic people and an undeniably industrial time can achieve something more than an "age" of high personal cultivation, there is something deeply defective in its culture. Such an age would be American in a topographical sense, not in a spiritual one.

This fact gives significance to the question so often raised as to whether the material and mechanistic forces of the machine age are to crush the higher life. In one sense I find, as I have already said, no special danger. Poets, painters, novelists, dramatists, philosophers, scientists, are sure to appear and to find an appreciative audience. But the unique fact about our own civilization is that if it is to achieve and manifest a characteristic culture, it must develop, not on top of an industrial and political substructure, but out of our material civilization itself. It will come by turning a machine age into a significantly new habit of mind and sentiment, or it will not come at all. A cultivation of a class that externally adorns a material civilization will at most merely repeat the sort of thing that has transiently happened many times before.

The question, then, is not merely a quantitative one. It is not a matter of an increased number of persons who will take part in the creation and enjoyment of art and science. It is a qualitative question. Can a material, industrial civilization be converted into a distinctive agency for liberating the minds and refining the emotions of all who take part in it? The cultural question is a political and economic one before it is a definitely cultural one.

It is a commonplace that the problem of the relation of mechanistic and industrial civilization to culture is the deepest and most urgent problem of our day. If interpreters are correct in saying that "Americanization" is becoming universal, it is a problem of the world and not just of our own country—although it is first acutely experienced here. It raises issues of the widest philosophic import. The question of the relation of man and nature, of mind and matter, assumes its vital significance in this context. A "humanism" that separates man from nature will envisage a radically different solution of the industrial and economic perplexities of the age than the humanism entertained by those who find no uncrossable gulf or fixed gap. The former will inevitably look backward for direction; it will strive for a cultivated élite supported on the backs of toiling masses. The latter will have to face the question of whether work itself can become an instrument of culture and of how the masses can share freely in a life enriched in imagination and esthetic enjoyment. This task is set not because of sentimental "humanitarianism," but as the necessary conclusion of the intellectual conviction that while man belongs in nature and mind is connected with matter, humanity and its collective intelligence are the means by which nature is guided to new possibilities.

Many European critics openly judge American life from the standpoint of a dualism of the spiritual and material, and deplore the primacy of the physical as fatal to any culture. They fail to see the depth and range of our problem, which is that of making the material an active instrument in the creation of the life of ideas and art. Many American critics of the present scene are engaged in devising modes of escape. Some flee to Paris or Florence; others take flight in their imagination to India, Athens, the Middle Ages or the American age of Emerson, Thoreau and Melville. Flight is solution by evasion. Return to a dualism consisting of a massive substratum of the material upon which are erected spiritually ornamented façades, is flatly impossible, except upon the penalty of the spiritual disenfranchisement of those permanently condemned to toil mechanically at the machine.

That the cultural problem must be reached through economic roads is testified to by our educational system. No nation has ever been so actively committed to universal schooling as are the people of the United States. But what is our system for? What ends does it serve? That it gives opportunity to many who would otherwise lack it is undeniable. It is also the agency of important welding and fusing processes. These are conditions of creation of a mind that will constitute a distinctive type of culture. But they are conditions only. If our public-school system merely turns out efficient industrial fodder and citizenship fodder in a state controlled by pecuniary industry, as other schools in other nations have turned out efficient cannon fodder, it is not helping to solve the problem of building up a distinctive American culture; it is only aggravating the problem. That which prevents the schools from doing their educational work freely is precisely the pressure—for the most part indirect, to be sure—of domination by the money-motif of our economic regime. The subject is too large to deal with here. But the distinguishing trait of the American student body in our higher schools is a kind of intellectual immaturity. This immaturity is mainly due to their enforced mental seclusion; there is, in their schooling, little free and disinterested concern with the underlying social problems of our civilization. Other typical evidence is found in the training of engineers. Thorstein Veblen—and many others have since repeated his idea—pointed out the strategic position occupied by the engineer in our industrial and technological activity. Engineering schools give excellent technical training. Where is the school that pays systematic attention to the potential social function of the engineering profession?

I refer to the schools in connection with this problem of American culture because they are the formal agencies for producing those mental attitudes, those modes of feeling and thinking, which are the essence of a distinctive culture. But they are not the ultimate formative force. Social institutions, the trend of occupations, the pattern of social arrangements, are the finally controlling influences in shaping minds. The immaturity nurtured in schools is carried over into life. If we Americans manifest, as compared with those of other countries who have had the benefits of higher schooling, a kind of infantilism, it is because our own schooling so largely evades serious consideration of the deeper issues of social life; for it is only through induction into realities that mind can be matured. Consequently the effective education, that which really leaves a stamp on character and thought, is obtained when graduates come to take their part in the activities of an adult society which put exaggerated emphasis upon business and the results of business success. Such an education is at best extremely one-sided; it operates to create the specialized "business mind," and this, in turn, is manifested in leisure as well as in business itself. The one-sidedness is accentuated because of the tragic irrelevancy of prior schooling to the controlling realities of social life. There is little preparation to induce either hardy resistance, discriminating criticism, or the vision and desire to direct economic forces in new channels.

If, then, I select education for special notice, it is because education—in the broad sense of formation of fundamental attitudes of imagination, desire and thinking—is strictly correlative with culture in its inclusive social sense. It is because the educative influence of economic and political institutions is, in the last analysis, even more important than their immediate economic consequences. The mental poverty that comes from one-sided distortion of mind is ultimately more significant than poverty in material goods. To make this assertion is not to gloss over the material harshness that exists. It is rather to point out that under present conditions these material results cannot be separated from development of mind and character. Destitution on the one side and wealth on the other are factors in the determination of that psychological and moral constitution which is the source and the measure of attained culture. I can think of nothing more childishly futile, for example, than the attempt t bring "art" and esthetic enjoyment externally to the multitudes who work in the ugliest surroundings and who leave their ugly factories only to go through depressing streets to eat, sleep and carry on their domestic occupations in grimy, sordid homes. The interest of the younger generation in ait and esthetic matters is a hopeful sign of the growth of culture in its narrower sense. But it will readily turn into an escape mechanism unless it develops into an alert interest in the conditions which determine the esthetic environment of the vast multitudes who now live, work and play in surroundings that perforce degrade their tastes and that unconsciously educate them into desire for any kind of enjoyment as long as it is cheap and "exciting."

It is the work of sociologists, psychologists, novelists, dramatists and poets to exhibit the consequences of our present economic regime upon taste, desire, satisfaction and standards of value. An article like this cannot do a work which requires many volumes. But a paragraph suffices to call attention to one central fact. Most of those who are engaged in the outward work of production and distribution of economic commodities have no share—imaginative, intellectual, emotional—in directing the activities in which they physically participate.

It was remarked in an earlier chapter that there is definite restriction placed upon existing corporateness. It is found in the fact that economic associations are fixed in ways which exclude most of the workers in them from taking part in their management. The subordination of the enterprises to pecuniary profit reacts to make the workers "hands" only. Their hearts and brains are not engaged. They execute plans which they do not form, and of whose meaning and intent they are ignorant—beyond the fact that these plans make a profit for others and secure a wage for themselves. To set forth the consequences of this fact upon the experience and the minds of uncounted multitudes would again require volumes. But there is an undeniable limitation of opportunities, and minds are warped, frustrated, unnourished by their activities—the ultimate source of all constant nurture of the spirit. The philosopher's idea of a complete separation of mind and body is realized in thousands of industrial workers, and the result is a depressed body and an empty and distorted mind.

There are instances, here and there, of the intellectual and moral effects which accrue when workers can employ their feelings and imaginations as well as their muscles in what they do. But it is still impossible to foresee in detail what would happen if a system of cooperative control of industry were generally substituted for the present system of exclusion. There would be an enormous liberation of mind, and the mind thus set free would have constant direction and nourishment. Desire for related knowledge, physical and social, would be created and rewarded; initiative and responsibility would be demanded and achieved. One may not, perhaps, be entitled to predict that an efflorescence of a distinctive social culture would immediately result. But one can say without hesitation that we shall attain only the personal cultivation of a class, and not a characteristic American culture, unless this condition is fulfilled. It is impossible for a highly industrialized society to attain a widespread high excellence of mind when multitudes are excluded from occasion for the use of thought and emotion in their daily occupations. The contradiction is so great and so pervasive that a favorable issue is hopeless. We must wrest our general culture from an industrialized civilization; and this fact signifies that industry must itself become a primary educative and cultural force for those engaged in it. The conception that natural science somehow sets a limit to freedom, subjecting men to fixed necessities, is not an intrinsic product of science. Just as with the popular notion that art is a luxury, whose proper abode is the museum and gallery, the notion of literary persons (including some philosophers) that science is an oppression due to the material structure of nature, is ultimately a reflex of the social conditions under which science is applied so as to reach only a pecuniary fruition. Knowledge takes effect in machinery and in the minds of technical directors, but not in the thoughts of those who tend the machines. The alleged fatalism of science is in reality the fatalism of the pecuniary order in which science is employed.

If I have emphasized the effect upon the wage workers, it is not because the consequences are not equally marked with respect to the few who now enjoy the material emoluments of the system and monopolize its management and control. There will doubtless always be leaders, those who will have the more active and leading share in the intellectual direction of great industrial undertakings. But as long as the direction is more concerned with pecuniary profit than with social utility, the resulting intellectual and moral development will be one-sided and warped. An inevitable result of a cooperatively shared control of industry would be the recognition of final use or consumption as the criterion of valuation, decision and direction. When the point of view of consumption is supreme in industry, the latter will be socialized, and I see no way of securing its genuine socialization save as industry is viewed and conducted from the standpoint of the user and enjoyer of services and commodities. For then human values will control economic values. Moreover, as long as means are kept separate from human ends (the consequences produced in human living), "values in use" will be so dominated by exchange or sale values that the former will be interpreted by means of the latter. In other words, there is now no inherent criterion for consumption-values. "Wealth," as Ruskin so vehemently pointed out, includes as much *illth* as well-being. When values in use are the ends of industry they will receive a scrutiny and criticism for which there is no foundation at present, save external moralizing and exhortation. Production for private profit signifies that any kind of consumption will be stimulated that leads to private gain.

There can be no stable and balanced development of mind and character apart from the assumption of responsibility. In an industrialized society, that responsibility must for the most part be associated with industry, since it will grow indirectly out of industry even for those not engaged in it. The wider and fuller the sense of social consequences—that is, of the effect on the life-experience of the consumer—the deeper and surer, the more stable, is the intelligence of those who have the foremost place in the direction of industry. A society saturated with industrialism may evolve a class of highly cultivated persons in the traditional sense of cultivation. But there will be something thin and meagre about even this meed of cultivation if it evolves in isolation from the main currents of action in which thought and desire are engaged. As long as imagination is concerned primarily with obtaining pecuniary success and enjoying its material results, the type of culture will conform to these standards.

Everywhere and at all times the development of mind and its cultural products have been connate with the channels in which mind is exercised and applied. This fact defines the problem of creating a culture that will be characteristically our own. Escape from industrialism on the ground that it is unesthetic and brutal can win only a superficial and restricted success of esteem. It is a silly caricature to interpret such statements as meaning that science should devote itself directly to solving industrial problems, or that poetry and painting should find their material in machines and in machine processes. The question is not one of idealizing present conditions in esthetic treatment, but of discovering and trying to realize the conditions under which vital esthetic production and esthetic appreciation may take place on a generous social scale.

And similarly for science; it is not in the least a matter of considering this and that particular practical application to be squeezed out of science; we have a great deal of that sort of thing already. It is a question of acknowledgment on the part of scientific inquirers of intellectual responsibility; of admitting into their consciousness a perception of what science has actually done, through its counterpart technologies, in making the world and life what they are. This perception would bear fruit by raising the question of what science can do in making a different sort of world and society. Such a science would be at the opposite pole to science conceived as merely a means to special industrial ends. It would, indeed, include in its scope all the technological aspects of the latter, but it would also be concerned with control of their social effects. A humane society would use scientific method, and intelligence with its best equipment, to bring about human consequences. Such a society would meet the demand for a science that is humanistic, and not just physical and technical. "Solutions" of the problem of the relation of the material and the spiritual, of the ideal and the actual, are merely conceptual and at best prophetic unless material conditions are idealized by contributing to cultural consequences. Science is a potential tool of such a liberating spiritualization; the arts, including that of social control, are its fruition.

I do not hold, I think, an exaggerated opinion of the influence that is wielded by so-called "intellectuals"—philosophers, professional and otherwise, critics, writers and professional persons in general having interests beyond their immediate callings. But their present position is not a measure of their possibilities. For they are now intellectually dispersed and divided; this fact is one aspect of what I have called "the lost individual." This internal dissolution is necessarily accompanied by a weak social efficacy. The chaos is due, more than to anything else, to mental withdrawal, to the failure to face the realities of industrialized society. Whether the ultimate influence of the distinctively intellectual or reflective groups is to be great or small, an initial move is theirs. A consciously directed critical consideration of the state of present society in its causes and consequences is a pre-condition of projection of constructive ideas. To be effective, the movement must be organized. But this requirement does not demand the creation of a formal organization; it does demand that a sense of the need and opportunity should possess a sufficiently large number of minds. If it does, the results of their inquiries will converge to a common issue.

This point of view is sometimes represented as a virtual appeal to those primarily engaged in inquiry and reflection to desert their studies, libraries and laboratories and engage in works of social reform. That representation is a caricature. It is not the abandonment of thinking and inquiry that is asked for, but more thinking and more significant inquiry. This "more" is equivalent to a conscious direction of thought and inquiry, and direction can be had only by a realization of problems in the rank of their urgency. The "clerk" and secretary once occupied, if we may trust history, places of great influence if not of honor. In a society of military and political leaders who were illiterate, they must have done much of the thinking and negotiating for which the names of the great now receive credit. The intellectuals of the present are their descendants. Outwardly they have been emancipated and have an independent position formerly lacking. Whether their actual efficacy has been correspondingly increased may be doubted. In some degree, they have attained their liberty in direct ratio to their distance from the scenes of action. A more intimate connection would not signify, I repeat, a surrender of the business of thought, even speculative thought, for the sake of getting busy at some so-called practical matter. Rather would it signify a focussing of thought and intensifying of its quality by bringing it into relation with issues of stupendous meaning.

I am suspicious of all attempts to erect a hierarchy of values: their results generally prove to be inapplicable and abstract. But there is at every time a hierarchy of problems, for there are some issues which underlie and condition others. No one person is going to evolve a constructive solution for the problem of humanizing industrial civilization, of making it and its technology a servant of human life—a problem which is once more equivalent, for us, to that of creating a genuine culture. But general guidance of serious intellectual endeavor by a consciousness of the problem would enable at least one group of individuals to recover a social function and so refind themselves. And recovery by those with special intellectual gifts and equipment from their enforced social defection is at least a first step in a more general reconstruction that will bring integration out of disorder.

Accordingly, I do not wish my remarks about escape and withdrawal to be interpreted as if they were directed at any special group of persons. The flight of particular individuals is symptomatic of the seclusion of existing science, intelligence and art.

The personal gap which, generally speaking, isolates the intellectual worker from the wage earner is symbolic and typical of a deep division of functions. This division is the split between theory and practice in actual operation. The effects of the split are as fatal to culture on the one side as on the other. It signifies that what we call our culture will continue to be, and in increased measure, a survival of inherited European traditions, and that it will not be indigenous. And if it is true, as some hold, that with the extension of machine technology and industrialism the whole world is becoming "Americanized," then the creation of an indigenous culture is no disservice to the traditional European springs of our spiritual life. It will signify, not ingratitude, but the effort to repay a debt.

The solution of the crisis in culture is identical with the recovery of composed, effective and creative individuality. The harmony of individual mind with the realities of a civilization made outwardly corporate by an industry based on technology does not signify that individual minds will be passively molded by existing social conditions as if the latter were fixed and static. When the patterns that form individuality of thought and desire are in line with actuating social forces, that individuality will be released for creative effort. Originality and uniqueness are not opposed to social nurture; they are saved by it from eccentricity and escape. The positive and constructive energy of individuals, as manifested in the remaking and redirection of social forces and conditions, is itself a social necessity. A new culture expressing the possibilities immanent in a machine and material civilization will release whatever is distinctive and potentially creative in individuals, and individuals thus freed will be the constant makers of a continuously new society.

It was said in an earlier chapter that "acceptance" of conditions has two very different meanings. To this statement may now be added the consideration that "conditions" are always moving; they are always in transition to something else. The important question is whether intelligence, whether observation and reflection, intervenes and becomes a directive factor in the transition. The moment it does intervene, conditions become conditions of forecasting consequences; when these consequences present themselves in thought, preference and volition, planning and determination, come into play. To foresee consequences of existing conditions is to surrender neutrality and drift; it is to take sides in behalf of the consequences that are preferred. The cultural consequences that our industrial system now produces have no finality about them. When they are observed and are related discriminatingly to their causes, they become conditions for planning, desiring, choosing. Discriminating inquiry will disclose what part of present results is the outcome of the technological factors at work and what part is due to a legal and economic system which it is within the power of man to modify and transform. It is indeed foolish to assume that an industrial civilization will somehow automatically, from its own inner impetus, produce a new culture. But it is a lazy abdication of responsibility which assumes that a genuine culture can be achieved except first by an active and alert intellectual recognition of the realities of an industrial age, and then by planning to use them in behalf of a significantly human life. To charge that those who urge intellectual acknowledgment or acceptance as the first necessary step stop at this point, and thus end with an optimistic rationalization of the present as if it were final, is a misconstruction that indicates a desire to shirk responsibility for undertaking the task of reconstruction and direction. Or else it waits upon a miracle to beget the culture which is desired by all serious minds.

8. INDIVIDUALITY IN OUR DAY

In the foregoing chapters, I have attempted to portray the split between the idea of the individual inherited from the past and the realities of a situation that is becoming increasingly corporate. Some of the effects produced on living individuality by this division have been indicated. I have urged that individuality will again become integral and vital when it creates a frame for itself by attention to the scene in which it must perforce exist and develop. It is likely that many persons will regard my statement of the problem as a commonplace. Others will deplore my failure to offer a detailed solution and a definite picture of just what an individual would be if he were in harmony with the realities of American civilization. Still others will think that a disease has been described as a remedy; that the articles are an indiscriminate praise of technological science and of a corporate industrial civilization; that they are an effort to boost upon the bandwagon those reluctant to climb.

I have indeed attempted analysis, rather than either a condemnation of the evils of present society or a recommendation of fixed ends and ideals for their cure. For I think that serious minds are pretty well agreed as to both evils and ideals—as long as both are taken in general terms. Condemnation is too often only a way of displaying superiority; it speaks from outside the scene; it discloses symptoms but not causes. It is impotent to produce; it can only reproduce its own kind. As for ideals, all agree that we want the good life, and that the good life involves freedom and a taste that is trained to appreciate the honorable, the true and the beautiful. But as long as we limit ourselves to generalities, the phrases that express ideals may be transferred from conservative to radical or vice versa, and nobody will be the wiser. For, without analysis, they do not descend into the actual scene nor concern themselves with the generative conditions of realization of ideals.

There is danger in the reiteration of eternal verities and ultimate spiritualities. Our sense of the actual is dulled, and we are led to think that in dwelling upon ideal goals we have somehow transcended existing evils. Ideals express possibilities; but they are genuine ideals only in so far as they are possibilities of what is now moving. Imagination can set them free from their encumbrances and project them as a guide in attention to what now exists. But, save as they are related to actualities, they are pictures in a dream.

I have, then, ventured to suppose that analysis of present conditions is of primary importance. Analysis of even a casual kind discloses that these conditions are not fixed. To accept them intellectually is to perceive that they are in flux. Their movement is not destined to a single end. Many outcomes may be projected, and the movement may be directed by many courses to many chosen goals, once conditions have been recognized for what they are. By becoming conscious of their movements and by active participation in their currents, we may guide them to some preferred possibility. In this interaction, individuals attain an integrated being. The individual who intelligently and actively partakes in a perception that is a first step in conscious choice is never so isolated as to be lost nor so quiescent as to be suppressed.

One of the main difficulties in understanding the present and apprehending its human possibilities is the persistence of stereotypes of spiritual life which were formed in old and alien cultures. In static societies—those which the industrial revolution has doomed—acquiescence had a meaning, and so had the projection of fixed ideals. Things were so relatively settled that there was something to acquiesce in, and goals and ideals could be imagined that were as fixed in their way as existing conditions in theirs. The medieval legal system could define "just" prices and wages, for the definition was a formulation of what was customary in the local community; it operated merely to prevent exorbitant deviations. It could prescribe a system of definite duties for all relations, for there was a hierarchical order, and occasions for the exercise of duty fell within an established and hence known order. Communities were local; they did not merge, overlap and interact in all kinds of subtle and hidden ways. A common church was the guardian and administrator of spiritual and ideal truth, and its theoretical authority had direct channels for making itself felt in the practical details of life. Spiritual realities might have their locus in the next world, but this after-world was intimately tied into all the affairs of this world by an institution existing here and now.

To-day there are no patterns sufficiently enduring to provide anything stable in which to acquiesce, and there is no material out of which to frame final and all-inclusive ends. There is, on the other hand, such constant change that acquiescence is but a series of interrupted spasms, and the outcome is mere drifting. In such a situation, fixed and comprehensive goals are but irrelevant dreams, while acquiescence is not a policy but its abnegation.

Again, the machine is condemned wholesale because it is seen through the eyes of a spirituality that belonged to another state of culture. Present evil consequences are treated as if they were eternally necessary, because they cannot be made consistent with the ideals of another age. In reality, a machine age is a challenge to generate new conceptions of the ideal and the spiritual. Ferrero has said that machines "are the barbarians of modern times, which have destroyed the fairest works of ancient civilisations." But even the barbarians were not immutably barbarous; they, too, were bearers of directive movement, and in time they wrought out a civilization that had its own measure of fairness and beauty.

Most attacks on the mechanistic character of science are caused by the survival of philosophies and religions formed when nature was the grim foe of man. The possibility of the present, and therefore its problem, is that through and by science, nature may become the friend and ally of man. I have rarely seen an attack on science as hostile to humanism which did not rest upon a conception of nature formed long before there was any science. That there is much at any time in environing nature which is indifferent and hostile to human values is obvious to any serious mind. When natural knowledge was hardly existent, control of nature was impossible. Without power of control, there was no recourse save to build places of refuge in which man could live in imagination, although not in fact. There is no need to deny the grace and beauty of some of these constructions. But when their imaginary character is once made apparent, it is futile to suppose that men can go on living and sustaining life by them. When they are appealed to for support, the possibilities of the present are not perceived, and its constructive potentialities remain unutilized.

In reading many of the literary appreciations of science, one would gather that until the rise of modern science, men had not been aware that living in nature entails death and renders fortune precarious and uncertain; "science" is even treated as if it were responsible for the revelation of the fact that nature is often a foe of human interests and goods. But the very nature of the creeds that men have entertained in the past and of the rites they have practiced is proof that men were overwhelmingly conscious of this fact. If they had not been, they would not have resorted to magic, miracles, myth and the consolations and compensations of another world and life. As long as these things were sincerely believed in, dualism, anti-naturalism, had a meaning, for the "other world" was then a reality. To surrender the belief and retain the dualism is temporarily possible for bewildered minds. It is a condition which it is impossible to maintain permanently. The alternative is to accept what science tells us of the world in which we live and to resolve to use the agencies it puts within our power to render nature more amenable to human desire and more contributory to human good. "Naturalism" is a word with all kinds of meanings. But a naturalism which perceives that man with his habits, institutions, desires, thoughts, aspirations, ideals and struggles, is within nature, an integral part of it, has the philosophical foundation and the practical inspiration for effort to employ nature as an ally of human ideals and goods such as no dualism can possibly provide.

There are those who welcome science provided it remain "pure"; they see that as a pursuit and contemplated object it is an addition to the enjoyed meaning of life. But they feel that its applications in mechanical inventions are the cause of many of the troubles of modern society. Undoubtedly these applications have brought new modes of unloveliness and suffering. I shall not attempt the impossible task of trying to strike a net balance of ills and enjoyments between the days before and after the practical use of science. The significant point is that application is still restricted. It touches our dealings with things but not with one another. We use scientific method in directing physical but not human energies. Consideration of the full application of science must accordingly be prophetic rather than a record of what has already taken place. Such prophecy is not however without foundation. Even as things are there is a movement in science which foreshadows, if its inherent promise be carried out, a more humane age. For it looks forward to a time when all individuals may share in the discoveries and thoughts of others, to the liberation and enrichment of their own experience.

No scientific inquirer can keep what he finds to himself or turn it to merely private account without losing his scientific standing. Everything discovered belongs to the community of workers. Every new idea and theory has to be submitted to this community for confirmation and test. There is an expanding community of cooperative effort and of truth. It is true enough that these traits are now limited to small groups having a somewhat technical activity. But the existence of such groups reveals a possibility of the present—one of the many possibilities that are a challenge to expansion, and not a ground for retreat and contraction.

Suppose that what now happens in limited circles were extended and generalized. Would the outcome be oppression or emancipation? Inquiry is a challenge, not a passive conformity; application is a means of growth, not of repression. The general adoption of the scientific attitude in human affairs would mean nothing less than a revolutionary change in morals, religion, politics and industry. The fact that we have limited its use so largely to technical matters is not a reproach to science, but to the human beings who use it for private ends and who strive to defeat its social application for fear of destructive effects upon their power and profit. A vision of a day in which the natural sciences and the technologies that flow from them are used as servants of a humane life constitutes the imagination that is relevant to our own time. A humanism that flees from science as an enemy denies the means by which a liberal humanism might become a reality.

The scientific attitude is experimental as well as intrinsically communicative. If it were generally applied, it would liberate us from the heavy burden imposed by dogmas and external standards. Experimental method is something other than the use of blow-pipes, retorts and reagents. It is the foe of every belief that permits habit and wont to dominate invention and discovery, and ready-made system to override verifiable fact. Constant revision is the work of experimental inquiry. By revision of knowledge and ideas, power to effect transformation is given us. This attitude, once incarnated in the individual mind, would find an operative outlet. If dogmas and institutions tremble when a new idea appears, this shiver is nothing to what would happen if the idea were armed with the means for the continuous discovery of new truth and the criticism of old belief. To "acquiesce" in science is dangerous only for those who would maintain affairs in the existing social order unchanged because of lazy habit or self-interest. For the scientific attitude demands faithfulness to whatever is discovered and steadfastness in adhering to new truth.

The "given" which science calls upon us to accept is not fixed; it is in process. A chemist does not study the elements in order to bow down before them; ability to produce transformations is the outcome. It is said, and truly, that we are now oppressed by the weight of science. But why? Some allowance has to be made, of course, for the time it takes to learn the uses of new means and to appropriate their potentialities. When these means are as radically new as is experimental science, the time required is correspondingly long. But aside from this fact, the multiplication of means and materials is an increase of opportunities and purposes. It marks a release of individuality for affections and deeds more congenial to its own nature. Even the derided bathtub has its individual uses; an individual is not perforce degraded because he has the chance to keep himself clean. The radio will make for standardization and regimentation only as long as individuals refuse to exercise the selective reaction that is theirs. The enemy is not material commodities, but the lack of the will to use them as instruments for achieving preferred possibilities. Imagine a society free from pecuniary domination, and it becomes self-evident that material commodities are invitations to individual taste and choice, and occasions for individual growth. If human beings are not strong and steadfast enough to accept the invitation and take advantage of the proffered occasion, let us put the blame where it belongs.

There is at least this much truth in economic determinism. Industry is not outside of human life, but within it. The genteel tradition shuts its eyes to this fact; emotionally and intellectually it pushes industry and its material phase out into a region remote from human values. To stop with mere emotional rejection and moral condemnation of industry and trade as materialistic is to leave them in this inhuman region where they operate as the instruments of those who employ them for private ends. Exclusion of this sort is an accomplice of the forces that keep things in the saddle. There is a subterranean partnership between those who employ the existing economic order for selfish pecuniary gain and those who turn their backs upon it in the interest of personal complacency, private dignity, and irresponsibility.

Every occupation leaves its impress on individual character and modifies the outlook on life of those who carry it on. No one questions this fact as respects wage-earners tied to the machine, or business men who devote themselves to pecuniary manipulations. Callings may have their roots in innate impulses of human nature but their pursuit does not merely "express" these impulses, leaving them unaltered; their pursuit determines intellectual horizons, precipitates knowledge and ideas, shapes desire and interest. This influence operates in the case of those who set up fine art, science, or religion as ends in themselves, isolated from radiation and expansion into other concerns (such radiation being what "application" signifies) as much as in the case of those who engage in industry. The alternatives are lack of application with consequent narrowing and overspecialization, and application with enlargement and increase of liberality. The narrowing in the case of industry pursued apart from social ends is evident to all thoughtful persons. Intellectual and literary folks who conceive themselves devoted to pursuit of pure truth and uncontaminated beauty too readily overlook the fact that a similar narrowing and hardening takes place in them. Their goods are more refined, but they are also engaged in acquisition; unless they are concerned with use, with expansive interactions, they too become monopolists of capital. And the monopolization of spiritual capital may in the end be more harmful than that of material capital.

The destructive effect of science upon beliefs long cherished and values once prized is, and quite naturally so, a great cause of dread of science and its applications in life. The law of inertia holds of the imagination and its loyalties as truly as of physical things. I do not suppose that it is possible to turn suddenly from these negative effects to possible positive and constructive ones.

But as long as we refuse to make an effort to change the direction in which imagination looks at the world, as long as we remain unwilling to reexamine old standards and values, science will continue to wear its negative aspect. Take science (including its application to the machine) for what it is, and we shall begin to envisage it as a potential creator of new values and ends. We shall have an intimation, on a wide and generous scale, of the release, the increased initiative, independence and inventiveness, which science now brings in its own specialized fields to the individual scientist. It will be seen as a means of originality and individual variation. Even to those sciences which delight in calling themselves "pure," there is a significant lesson in the instinct that leads us to speak of Newton's and Einstein's law.

Because the free working of mind is one of the greatest joys open to man, the scientific attitude, incorporated in individual mind, is something which adds enormously to one's enjoyment of existence. The delights of thinking, of inquiry, are not widely enjoyed at the present time. But the few who experience them would hardly exchange them for other pleasures. Yet they are now as restricted in quality as they are in the number of those who share them. That is to say, as long as "scientific" thinking confines itself to technical fields, it lacks full scope and varied material. Its subject-matter is technical in the degree in which application in human life is shut out. The mind that is hampered by fear lest something old and precious be destroyed is the mind that experiences fear of science. He who has this fear cannot find reward and peace in the discovery of new truths and the projection of new ideals. He does not walk the earth freely, because he is obsessed by the need of protecting some private possession of belief and taste. For the love of private possessions is not confined to material goods.

It is a property of science to find its opportunities in problems, in questions. Since knowing is inquiring, perplexities and difficulties are the meat on which it thrives. The disparities and conflicts that give rise to problems are not something to be dreaded, something to be endured with whatever hardihood one can command; they are things to be grappled with. Each of us experiences these difficulties in the sphere of his personal relations, whether in his more immediate contacts or in the wider associations conventionally called "society." At present, personal frictions are one of the chief causes of suffering. I do not say all suffering would disappear with the incorporation of scientific method into individual disposition; but I do say that it is now immensely increased by our disinclination to treat these frictions as problems to be dealt with intellectually. The distress that comes from being driven in upon ourselves would be largely relieved; it would in part be converted into the enjoyment that attends the free working of mind, if we took them as occasions for the exercise of thought, as problems having an objective direction and outlet.

We all experience, as I have said, the perplexities that arise in the intimacies of personal intercourse. The more remote relations of society also present their troubles. There is much talk of "social problems." But we rarely treat them as problems in the intellectual sense of that word. They are thought of as "evils" needing correction; as naughty or diabolic things to be "reformed." Our preoccupation with these ideas is proof of how far we are from taking the scientific attitude. I do not say that the attitude of the physician who regards his patient as a "beautiful case" is wholly ideal. But it is more wholesome and more promising than the persistence of the pre-scientific habit of anxious concerns with evils and their reform. The current way of treating criminality and criminals is, for example, reminiscent of the way in which diseases were once thought of and dealt with. Their origin was once believed to be moral and personal; some enemy, diabolic or human, was thought to have injected some alien substance or force into the person who was ailing. The possibility of effective treatment began when diseases were regarded as having an intrinsic origin in interactions of the organism and its natural environment. We are only just beginning to think of criminality as an equally intrinsic manifestation of interactions between an individual and the social environment. With respect to it, and with respect to so many other evils, we persist in thinking and acting in prescientific "moral" terms. This pre-scientific conception of "evil" is probably the greatest barrier that exists to that real reform which is identical with constructive remaking.

Because science starts with questions and inquiries it is fatal to all social system-making and programs of fixed ends. In spite of the bankruptcy of past systems of belief, it is hard to surrender our faith in system and in some wholesale belief. We continually reason as if the difficulty were in the particular system that has failed and as if we were on the point of now finally hitting upon one that is true as all the others were false. The real trouble is with the attitude of dependence upon any of them. Scientific method would teach us to break up, to inquire definitely and with particularity, to seek solutions in the terms of concrete problems as they arise. It is not easy to imagine the difference which would follow from the shift of thought to discrimination and analysis. Wholesale creeds and all-inclusive ideals are impotent in the face of actual situations; for doing always means the doing of something in particular. They are worse than impotent. They conduce to blind and vague emotional states in which credulity is at home, and where action, following the lead of overpowering emotion, is easily manipulated by the self-seekers who have kept their heads and wits. Nothing would conduce more, for example, to the elimination of war than the substitution of specific analysis of its causes for the wholesale love of "liberty, humanity, justice and civilization."

All of these considerations would lead to the conclusion that depression of the individual is the individual's own liability, were it not for the time it takes for a new principle to make its way deeply into individual mind on a large scale. But as time goes on, the responsibility becomes an individual one. For individuality is inexpugnable and it is of its nature to assert itself. The first move in recovery of an integrated individual is accordingly with the individual himself. In whatever occupation he finds himself and whatever interest concerns him, he is himself and no other, and he lives in situations that are in some respect flexible and plastic.

We are given to thinking of society in large and vague ways. We should forget "society" and think of law, industry, religion, medicine, politics, art, education, philosophy—and think of them in the plural. For points of contact are not the same for any two persons, and hence the questions which the interests and occupations pose are never twice the same. There is no contact so immutable that it will not yield at some point. All these callings and concerns are the avenues through which the world acts upon us and we upon the world. There is no society at large, no business in general. Harmony with conditions is not a single and monotonous uniformity, but a diversified affair requiring individual attack.

Individuality is inexpugnable because it is a manner of distinctive sensitivity, selection, choice, response and utilization of conditions. For this reason, if for no other, it is impossible to develop integrated individuality by any all-embracing system or program. No individual can make the determination for anyone else; nor can he make it for himself all at once and forever. A native manner of selection gives direction and continuity, but definite expression is found in changing occasions and varied forms. The selective choice and use of conditions have to be continually made and remade. Since we live in a moving world and change with our interactions in it, every act produces a new perspective that demands a new exercise of preference. If, in the long run, an individual remains lost, it is because he has chosen irresponsibility; and if he remains wholly depressed it is because he has chosen the course of easy parasitism.

Acquiescence, in the sense of drifting, is not something to be achieved; it is something to be overcome, something that is "natural" in the sense of being easy. But it assumes a multitude of forms, and Rotarian applause for present conditions is only one of these forms. A different form of submission consists in abandoning the values of a new civilization for those of the past. To assume the uniform of some dead culture is only another means of regimentation. True integration is to be found in relevancy to the present, in active response to conditions as they present themselves, in the effort to make them over according to some consciously chosen possibility.

Individuality is at first spontaneous and unshaped; it is a potentiality, a capacity of development. Even so, it is a unique manner of acting in and with a world of objects and persons. It is not something complete in itself, like a closet in a house or a secret drawer in a desk, filled with treasures that are waiting to be bestowed on the world. Since individuality is a distinctive way of feeling the impacts of the world and of showing a preferential bias in response to these impacts, it develops into shape and form only through interaction with actual conditions; it is no more complete in itself than is a painter's tube of paint without relation to a canvas. The work of art is the truly individual thing; and it is the result of the interaction of paint and canvas through the medium of the artist's distinctive vision and power. In its determination, the potential individuality of the artist takes on visible and enduring form. The imposition of individuality as something made in advance always gives evidence of a mannerism, not of a manner. For the latter is something original and creative; something formed in the very process of creation of other things.

The future is always unpredictable. Ideals, including that of a new and effective individuality, must themselves be framed out of the possibilities of existing conditions, even if these be the conditions that constitute a corporate and industrial age. The ideals take shape and gain a content as they operate in remaking conditions. We may, in order to have continuity of direction, plan a program of action in anticipation of occasions as they emerge. But a program of ends and ideals if kept apart from sensitive and flexible method becomes an encumbrance. For its hard and rigid character assumes a fixed world and a static individual; and neither of these things exists. It implies that we can prophesy the future—an attempt which terminates, as someone has said, in prophesying the past or in its reduplication.

The same Emerson who said that "society is everywhere in conspiracy against its members" also said, and in the same essay, "accept the place the divine providence has found for you, the society of your contemporaries, the connection of events." Now, when events are taken in disconnection and considered apart from the interactions due to the selecting individual, they conspire against individu-'ity. So does society when it is accepted as something already fixed in institutions. But "the connection of events," and "the society of your contemporaries" as formed of moving and multiple associations, are the only means by which the possibilities of individuality can be realized.

Psychiatrists have shown how many disruptions and dissipations of the individual are due to his withdrawal from reality into a merely inner world. There are, however, many subtle forms of retreat, some of which are erected into systems of philosophy and are glorified in current literature. "It is in vain," said Emerson, "that we look for genius to reiterate its miracles in the old arts; it is its instinct to find beauty and holiness in new and necessary facts, in the field and road-side, in the shop and mill." To gain an integrated individuality, each of us needs to cultivate his own garden. But there is no fence about this garden: it is no sharply marked-off enclosure. Our garden is the world, in the angle at which it touches our own manner of being. By accepting the corporate and industrial world in which we live, and by thus fulfilling the pre-condition for interaction with it, we, who are also parts of the moving present, create ourselves as we create an unknown future.

LIBERALISM AND SOCIAL ACTION

CONTENTS

1. THE HISTORY OF LIBERALISM

Liberalism has long been accustomed to onslaughts proceeding from those who oppose social change. It has long been treated as an enemy by those who wish to maintain the *status quo*. But today these attacks are mild in comparison with indictments proceeding from those who want drastic social changes effected in a twinkling of an eye, and who believe that violent overthrow of existing institutions is the right method of effecting the required changes. From current assaults, I select two as typical: "A liberal is one who gives up approval to the grievances of the proletariat, but who at the critical moment invariably runs to cover on the side of the masters of capitalism." Again, a liberal is defined as "one who professes radical opinions in private but who never acts upon them for fear of losing *entrée* into the courts of the mighty and respectable." Such statements might be cited indefinitely. They indicate that, in the minds of many persons, liberalism has fallen between two stools, so that it is conceived as the refuge of those unwilling to take a decided stand in the social conflicts going on. It is called mealy-mouthed, a milk-and-water doctrine and so on.

Popular sentiment, especially in this country, is subject to rapid changes of fashion. It was not a long time ago that liberalism was a term of praise; to be liberal was to be progressive, forward-looking, free from prejudice, characterized by all admirable qualities. I do not think, however, that this particular shift can be dismissed as a mere fluctuation of intellectual fashion. Three of the great nations of Europe have summarily suppressed the civil liberties for which liberalism valiantly strove, and in few countries of the Continent are they maintained with vigor. It is true that none of the nations in question has any long history of devotion to liberal ideals. But the new attacks proceed from those who profess they are concerned to change not to preserve old institutions. It is well known that everything for which liberalism stands is put in peril in times of war. In a world crisis, its ideals and methods are equally challenged; the belief spreads that liberalism flourishes only in times of fair social weather.

It is hardly possible to refrain from asking what liberalism really is; what elements, if any, of permanent value it contains, and how these values shall be maintained and developed in the conditions the world now faces. On my own account, I have raised these questions. I have wanted to find out whether it is possible for a person to continue, honestly and intelligently, to be a liberal, and if the answer be in the affirmative, what kind of liberal faith should be asserted today. Since I do not suppose that I am the only one who has put such questions to himself, I am setting forth the conclusions to which my examination of the problem has led me. If there is danger, on one side, of cowardice and evasion, there is danger on the other side of losing the sense of historic perspective and of yielding precipitately to short-time contemporary currents, abandoning in panic things of enduring and priceless value.

The natural beginning of the inquiry in which we are engaged is consideration of the origin and past development of liberalism. It is to this topic that the present chapter is devoted. The conclusion reached from a brief survey of history, namely, that liberalism has had a chequered career, and that it has meant in practice things so different as to be opposed to one another, might perhaps have been anticipated without prolonged examination of its past. But location and description of the ambiguities that cling to the career of liberalism will be of assistance in the attempt to determine its significance for today and tomorrow.

The use of the words liberal and liberalism to denote a particular social philosophy does not appear to occur earlier than the first decade of the nineteenth century. But the thing to which the words are applied is older. It might be traced back to Greek thought; some of its ideas, especially as to the importance of the free play of intelligence, may be found notably expressed in the funeral oration attributed to Pericles. But for the present purpose it is not necessary to go back of John Locke, the philosopher of the "glorious revolution" of 1688. The outstanding points of Locke's version of liberalism are that governments are instituted to protect the rights that belong to individuals prior to political organization of social relations. These rights are those summed up a century later in the American Declaration of Independence: the rights of life, liberty and the pursuit of happiness. Among the "natural" rights especially emphasized by Locke is that of property, originating, according to him, in the fact that an individual has "mixed" himself, through his labor, with some natural hitherto unappropriated object. This view was directed against levies on property made by rulers without authorization from the representatives of the people. The theory culminated in justifying the right of revolution. Since governments are instituted to protect the natural rights of individuals, they lose claim to obedience when they invade and destroy these rights instead of safeguarding them: a doctrine that well served the alms of our forefathers in their revolt against British rule, and that also found an extended application in the French Revolution of 1789.

The impact of this earlier liberalism is evidently political. Yet one of Locke's greatest interests was to uphold toleration in an age when intolerance was rife, persecution of dissenters in faith almost the rule, and when wars, civil and between nations, had a religious color. In serving the immediate needs of England—and then those of other countries in which it was desired to substitute representative for arbitrary government—it bequeathed to later social thought a rigid doctrine of natural rights inherent in individuals independent of social organization. It gave a directly practical import to the older semi-theological and semi-metaphysical conception of natural law as supreme over positive law and gave a new version of the old idea that natural law is the counterpart of reason, being disclosed by the natural light with which man is endowed.

The whole temper of this philosophy is individualistic in the sense in which individualism is opposed to organized social action. It held to the primacy of the individual over the state not only in time but in moral authority. It defined the individual in terms of liberties of thought and action already possessed by him in some mysterious ready-made fashion, and which it was the sole business of the state to safeguard. Reason was also made an inherent endowment of the individual, expressed in men's moral relations to one another, but not sustained and developed because of these relations. It followed that the great enemy of individual liberty was thought to be government because of its tendency to encroach upon the innate liberties of individuals. Later liberalism inherited this conception of a natural antagonism between ruler and ruled, interpreted as a natural opposition between the individual and organized society. There still lingers in the minds of some the notion that there are two different "spheres" of action and of rightful claims; that of political society and that of the individual, and that in the interest of the latter the former must be as contracted as possible. Not till the second half of the nineteenth century did the idea arise that government might and should be an instrument for securing and extending the liberties of individuals. This later aspect of liberalism is perhaps foreshadowed in the clauses of our Constitution that confer upon Congress power to provide for "public welfare" as well as for public safety.[1]

What has already been said indicates that with Locke the inclusion of the economic factor, property, among natural rights had a political animus. However, Locke at times goes so far as to designate as property everything that is included in "life, liberties and estates"; the individual has property in himself and in his life and activities; property in this broad sense is that which political society should protect. The importance attached to the right of property within the political area was

---

1. Probably in the minds of the framers of the Constitution not much more was contemplated by this clause than the desirability of permitting Congress to make appropriations for roads, rivers and harbors. In subsequent practice, the power has not been used much beyond provision of limited social services for those at an economic disadvantage.

without doubt an influence in the later definitely economic formulation of liberalism. But Locke was interested in property already possessed. A century later industry and commerce were sufficiently advanced in Great Britain so that interest centered in *production* of wealth, rather than in its possession. The conception of labor as the source of right in property was employed not so much to protect property from confiscation by the ruler (that right was practically secure in England) as to urge and justify freedom in the use and investment of capital and the right of laborers to move about and seek new modes of employment—claims denied by the common law that came down from semi-feudal conditions. The earlier economic conception may fairly be called static; it was concerned with possessions and estates. The newer economic conception was dynamic. It was concerned with release of productivity and exchange from a cumbrous complex of restrictions that had the force of law. The enemy was no longer the arbitrary special action of rulers. It was the whole system of common law and judicial practice in its adverse bearing upon freedom of labor, investment and exchange.

The transformation of earlier liberalism that took place because of this new interest is so tremendous that its story must be told in some detail. The concern for liberty and for the individual, which was the basis of Lockeian liberalism, persisted; otherwise the newer theory would not have been liberalism. But liberty was given a very different practical meaning. In the end, the effect was to subordinate political to economic activity; to connect natural laws with the laws of production and exchange, and to give a radically new significance to the earlier conception of reason. The name of Adam Smith is indissolubly connected with initiation of this transformation.

Although he was far from being an unqualified adherent of the idea of *laissez faire*, he held that the activity of individuals, freed as far as possible from political restriction, is the chief source of social welfare and the ultimate spring of social progress. He held that there is a "natural" or native tendency in every individual to better each his own estate through putting forth effort (labor) to satisfy his natural wants. Social welfare is promoted because the cumulative, but undesigned and unplanned, effect of the convergence of a multitude of individual efforts is to increase the commodities and services put at the disposal of men collectively, of society. This increase of goods and services creates new wants and leads to putting forth new modes of productive energy. There is not only a native impulse to exchange, to "truck," but individuals are released by the processes of exchange from the necessity for labor in order to satisfy all of the individual's own wants; through division of labor, productivity is enormously increased. Free economic processes thus bring about an endless spiral of ever increasing change, and through the guidance of an "invisible hand" (the equivalent of the doctrine of preestablished harmony so dear to the eighteenth century) the efforts of individuals for personal advancement and personal gain accrue to the benefit of society, and create a continuously closer knit interdependence of interests.

The ideas and ideals of the new political economy were congruous with the increase of industrial activity that was marked in England even before the invention of the steam engine. They spread rapidly. Their power was furthered when the great industrial and commercial expansion of England ensued in the wake of the substitution of mechanical for human energy, first in textiles and then in other occupations.

Under the influence of the industrial revolution the old argument against political action as a social agency assumed a new form. Such action was not only an invasion of individual liberty but it was in effect a conspiracy against the causes that bring about social progress. The Lockeian idea of natural laws took on a much more concrete, a more directly practical, meaning. Natural law was still regarded as something more fundamental than man-made law, which by comparison is artificial. But natural laws lost their remote moral meaning. They were identified with the laws of free industrial production and free commercial exchange. Adam Smith, however, did not originate this latter idea. He took it over from the French physiocrats, who, as the name implies, believed in rule of social relations by natural law and who identified natural with economic law.

France was an agricultural country, and the economy of the physiocrats was conceived and formulated in the interest of agriculture and mining. Land, according to them, is the source of all wealth; from it comes ultimately all genuinely productive force. Industry, as distinct from agriculture, merely reshapes what nature provides. The movement was essentially a protest against governmental measures that were impoverishing the agriculturalist and that enriched idle parasites. But its underlying philosophy was the idea that economic laws are the true natural laws while other laws are artificial and hence to be limited in scope as far as possible. In an ideal society political organization will be modeled upon the economic pattern set by nature. *Ex natura, jus.*

Locke had taught that labor, not land, is the source of wealth, and England was passing from an agrarian to an industrialized community. The French doctrine in its own form did not fit into the English scene. But there was no great obstacle against translating the underlying ideal of the identity of natural law with economic law into a form suited to the needs of an industrial community. The shift from land to labor (the expenditure of energy for the satisfaction of wants) required only, from the side of the philosophy of economics, that attention be centered upon human nature, rather than upon physical nature. Psychological laws, based on human nature, are as truly natural as are any laws based on land and physical nature. Land is itself productive only under the influence of the labor put forth in satisfaction of intrinsic human wants. Adam Smith was not himself especially interested in elaborating a formulation of laws in terms of human nature. But he explicitly fell back upon one natural human tendency, sympathy, to find the basis for morals, and he used other natural impulses, the instincts to better one's condition and to exchange, to give the foundation of economic theory. The laws of the operations of these natural tendencies, when they are freed from artificial restraints, are the natural laws governing men in their relations to one another. In individuals, the exercise of sympathy in accordance with reason (that is, in Smith's conception, from the standpoint of an impartial spectator) is the norm of virtuous action. But government cannot appeal to sympathy. The only measures it can employ affect the motive of self-interest. It makes this appeal most effectively when it acts so as to protect individuals in the exercise of their natural self-interest. These ideas, implicit in Smith, were made explicit by his successors: in part by the classical school of economists and in part by Bentham and the Mills, father and son. For a considerable period these two schools worked hand in hand.

Economists developed the principle of the free economic

activity of individuals; since this freedom was identified with absence of governmental action, conceived as an interference with natural liberty, the result was the formulation of *laissez faire* liberalism. Bentham carried the same conception, though from a different point of view, into a vigorous movement for reform of the common law and judicial procedure by means of legislative action. The Mills developed the psychological and logical foundation implicit in the theories of the economists and of Bentham.

I begin with Bentham. The existing legal system was intimately bound up with a political system based upon the predominance of the great landed proprietors through the rotten borough system. The operation of the new industrial forces in both production and exchange was checked and deflected at almost every point by a mass of customs that formed the core of common law. Bentham approached the situation not from the standpoint of individual liberty but from the standpoint of the effect of these restrictions upon the happiness enjoyed by individuals. Every restriction upon liberty is *ipso facto* a source of pain and a limitation of a pleasure that might otherwise be enjoyed. Hence the effect was the same in the two doctrines as far as the rightful province of governmental action is concerned. Bentham's assault was aimed directly, not indirectly, like the theory of the economists, upon everything in existing law and judicial procedure that inflicted unnecessary pain and that limited the acquisition of pleasures by individuals. Moreover, his psychology converted the impulse to improve one's condition, upon which Adam Smith had built, into the doctrine that desire for pleasure and aversion to pain are the sole forces that govern human action. The psychological theory implicit in the idea of industry and exchange controlled by desire for gain was then worked out upon the political and legal side. Moreover, the constant expansion of manufacturing and trade put the force of a powerful class interest behind the new version of liberalism. This statement does not imply that the intellectual leaders of the new liberalism were themselves moved by hope of material gain. On the contrary, they formed a group animated by a strikingly unselfish spirit, in contrast with their professed theories. Their very detachment from the immediate interests of the market place liberated them from the narrowness and shortsightedness that marked the trading class—a class that John Stuart Mill adverted to with even more bitterness than did Adam Smith. This emancipation enabled them to detect and make articulate the nascent movements of their time—a function that defines the genuine work of the intellectual class at any period. But they might have been as voices crying in the wilderness if what they taught had not coincided with the interests of a class that was constantly ris- ing in prestige and power.

According to Bentham, the criterion of all law and of every administrative effort is its effect upon the sum of happiness enjoyed by the greatest possible number. In calculating this sum, every individual is to count as one and only as one. The mere formulation of the doctrine was an attack upon every inequality of status that had the sanction of law. In effect, it made the well-being of the individual the norm of political action in every area in which it operates. In effect, though not wholly in Bentham's express apprehension, it transferred atten- tion from the well-being already possessed by individuals to one they might attain if there were a radical change in social insti- tutions. For existing institutions enabled a small number of individuals to enjoy their pleasures at the cost of the misery of a much greater number. While Bentham himself conceived that the changes to be made in legal and political institutions were mainly negative, such as abolition of abuses, corruptions and inequalities, nevertheless (as we shall see later) there was nothing in his fundamental doctrine that stood in the way of using the power of government to create, constructively and positively, new institutions if and when it should appear that the latter would contribute more effectively to the well-being of individuals.

Bentham's best known work is entitled *Principles of Morals and Legislation*. In his actual treatment "morals and legislation" form a single term. It was the morals *of* legislation, of political action generally, with which he occupied himself, his standard being the simple one of determination of its effect upon the greatest possible happiness of the greatest possible number. He labored incessantly to expose the abuses of the existing legal system and its application in judicial procedure, civil and criminal, and in administration. He attacked these abuses, in his various works, in detail, one by one. But his attacks were cumulative in effect since he applied a single principle in his detailed criticism. He was, we may say, the first great muck-raker in the field of law. But he was more than that. Wherever he saw a defect, he proposed a remedy. He was an inventor in law and administration, as much so as any contemporary in mechanical production. He said of himself that his ambition was to "extend the experimental method of reasoning from the physical branch to the moral"—meaning, in common with English thought of the eighteenth century, by the moral the human. He also compared his own work with what physicists and chemists were doing in their fields in invention of appliances and processes that increase human welfare. That is, he did not limit his method to mere reasoning; the latter occurred only for the sake of instituting changes in actual practice. History shows no mind more fertile than his invention of legal and administrative devices. Of him and his school, Graham Wallas said, "The fact that the fall from power of the British aristocracy in 1832 led neither to social revolution or administrative chaos at home, nor to the break up of the new British Empire abroad was largely due to the political expedients—local government reform, open competition in the civil service, scientific health and police administration, colonial self-government, Indian administrative reform—which Bentham's disciples either found in his writings, or developed, after his death, by his methods."[2]

The work of Bentham, in spite of fundamental defects in his underlying theory of human nature, is a demonstration that liberalism is not compelled by anything in its own nature to be impotent save for minor reforms. Bentham's influence is proof that liberalism can be a power in bringing about radical social changes:—provided it combine capacity for bold and comprehensive social invention with detailed study of particulars and with courage in action. The history of the legal and administrative changes in Great Britain during the first half of the nineteenth century is chiefly the history of Bentham and his school. I think there is something significant for the liberalism of today and tomorrow to be found in the fact that his group did not consist in any large measure of politicians, legislators or public officials. On the American principle of "Let George do it," liberals in this country are given to supposing and hoping that some Administration when in power will take the lead in

---

2. Article on Bentham in the *Encyclopaedia of the Social Sciences*, Vol. 11, p. 519.

formulating and executing liberal policies. I know of nothing in history that justifies the belief and hope. A liberal program has to be developed, and in a good deal of particularity, outside of the immediate realm of governmental action and enforced upon public attention, before direct political action of a thoroughgoing liberal sort will follow. This is one lesson we have to learn from early nineteenth-century liberalism. Without a background of informed political intelligence, direct action in behalf of professed liberal ends may end in development of political irresponsibility.

Bentham's theory led him to the view that all organized action is to be judged by its consequences, consequences that take effect in the lives of individuals. His psychology was rather rudimentary. It made him conceive of consequences as being atomic units of pleasures and pains that can be algebraically summed up. It is to this aspect of his doctrines that later writers, especially moralists, have chiefly devoted their critical attention. But this particular aspect of his theory, if we view it in the perspective of history, is an adventitious accretion. His enduring idea is that customs, institutions, laws, social arrangements are to be judged on the basis of their consequences as these come home to the individuals that compose society. Because of his emphasis upon consequences, he made short work of the tenets of both of the two schools that had dominated, before his day, English political thought. He brushed aside, almost contemptuously, the conservative school that found the source of social wisdom in the customs and precedents of the past. This school has its counterpart in those empiricists of the present day who attack every measure and policy that is new and innovating on the ground that it does not have the sanction of experience, when what they really mean by "experience" is patterns of mind that were formed in a past that no longer exists.

But Bentham was equally aggressive in assault upon that aspect of earlier liberalism which was based upon the conception of inherent natural rights—following in this respect a clew given by David Hume. Natural rights and natural liberties exist only in the kingdom of mythological social zoology. Men do not obey laws because they think these laws are in accord with a scheme of natural rights. They obey because they believe, rightly or wrongly, that the consequences of obeying are upon the whole better than the consequences of disobeying. If the consequences of existing rule become too intolerable, they revolt. An enlightened self-interest will induce a ruler not to push too far the patience of subjects. The enlightened self-interest of citizens will lead them to obtain by peaceful means, as far as possible, the changes that will effect a distribution of political power and the publicity that will lead political authorities to work for rather than against the interests of the people—a situation which Bentham thought was realized by government that is representative and based upon popular suffrage. But in any case, not natural rights but consequences in the lives of individuals are the criterion and measure of policy and judgment.

Because the liberalism of the economists and the Benthamites was adapted to contemporary conditions in Great Britain, the influence of the liberalism of the school of Locke waned. By 1820 it was practically extinct. Its influence lasted much longer in the United States. We had no Bentham and it is doubtful whether he would have had much influence if he had appeared. Except for movements in codification of law, it is hard to find traces of the influence of Bentham in this country. As was intimated earlier, the philosophy of Locke bore much the same relation to the American revolt of the colonies that it had to the British revolution of almost a century earlier. Up to, say, the time of the Civil War, the United States were predominantly agrarian. As they became industrialized, the philosophy of liberty of individuals, expressed especially in freedom of contract, provided the doctrine needed by those who controlled the economic system. It was freely employed by the courts in declaring unconstitutional legislation that limited this freedom. The ideas of Locke embodied in the Declaration of Independence were congenial to our pioneer conditions that gave individuals the opportunity to carve their own careers. Political action was lightly thought of by those who lived in frontier conditions. A political career was very largely annexed as an adjunct to the action of individuals in carving their own careers. The gospel of self-help and private initiative was practiced so spontaneously that it needed no special intellectual support. Finally, there was no background of feudalism to give special leverage to the Benthamite system of legal and administrative reform.

The United States lagged more than a generation behind Great Britain in promotion of social legislation. Justice Holmes found it necessary to remind his fellow justices that, after all, the *Social Statics* of Herbert Spencer had not been enacted into the American Constitution. Great Britain, largely under Benthamite influence, built up an ordered civil service independent of political party control. With us, political emoluments, like economic pecuniary rewards, went to the most enterprising competitor; to the victor belong the spoils. The principle of the greatest good to the greatest number tended to establish in Great Britain the supremacy of national over local interests. The political history of the United States is largely a record of domination by regional interests. Our fervor in law-making might be allied to Bentham's principle of the "omnicompetence" of the legislative body. But we have never taken very seriously the laws we make, while there has been little comparable in our history to the importance attached to administration by the English utilitarian school.

I have mentioned two schools of liberalism in Great Britain, that of the economists and of the utilitarians. At first they walked the same path. The later history of liberalism in that country is largely a matter of a growing divergence, and finally of an open split. While Bentham personally was on the side of the classical economists, his principle of judgment by consequences lends itself to opposite application. Bentham himself urged a great extension of public education and of action in behalf of public health. When he disallowed the doctrine of inalienable individual natural rights, he removed, as far as theory is concerned, the obstacle to positive action by the state whenever it can be shown that the general well-being will be promoted by such action. Dicey in his *Law and Opinion in England* has shown that collectivist legislative policies gained in force for at least a generation after the sixties. It was stimulated, naturally, by the reform bills that greatly broadened the basis of suffrage. The use of scientific method, even if sporadic and feeble, encouraged study of actual consequences and promoted the formation of legislative policies designed to improve the consequences brought about by existing institutions. At all events, in connection with Benthamite influence, it greatly weakened the notion that Reason is a remote majestic power that discloses ultimate truths. It tended to render it an agency in investigation of concrete situations and in projection of measures for their betterment.

I would not, however, give the impression that the trend

away from individualistic to collectivistic liberalism was the
direct effect of utilitarianism. On the contrary, social legislation
was fostered primarily by Tories, who, traditionally, had no
love for the industrialist class. Benthamite liberalism was not
the source of factory laws, laws for the protection of child and
women, prevention of their labor in mines, workmen's compensation acts, employers' liability laws, reduction of hours of
labor, the dole, and a labor code. All of these measures went
contrary to the idea of liberty of contract fostered by *laissez faire*
liberalism. Humanitarianism, in alliance with evangelical piety
and with romanticism, gave chief support, from the intellectual
and emotional side, to these measures, as the Tory party was
their chief political agent. No account of the rise of humani-
tarian sentiment as a force in creation of the new regulations
of industry would be adequate that did not include the names
of religious leaders drawn from both dissenters and the Established Church. Such names as Wilberforce, Clarkson, Zachary
Macaulay, Elizabeth Fry, Hannah More, as well as Lord Shaftes-
bury, come to mind. The trades unions were gaining power
and there was an active socialist movement, as represented by
Robert Owen. But in spite of, or along with, such movements,
we have to remember that liberalism is associated with generosity of outlook as well as with liberty of belief and action.
Gradually a change came over the spirit and meaning of liberalism. It came surely, if gradually, to be disassociated from the
laissez faire creed and to be associated with the use of governmental action for aid to those at economic disadvantage and
for alleviation of their conditions. In this country, save for a
small band of adherents to earlier liberalism, ideas and policies
of this general type have virtually come to define the meaning
of liberal faith. American liberalism as illustrated in the polit-

ical progressivism of the early present century has so little in common with British liberalism of the first part of the last century that it stands in opposition to it.

The influence of romanticism, as exemplified in different ways by Coleridge, Wordsworth, Carlyle and Ruskin, is worthy of especial note. These men were politically allied as a rule with the Tory party, if not actively, at least in sympathy. The romanticists were all of them vigorous opponents of the consequences of the industrialization of England, and directed their assaults at the economists and Benthamites whom they held largely responsible for these consequences. As against dependence upon uncoordinated individual activities, Coleridge emphasized the significance of enduring institutions. They, according to him, are the means by which men are held together in concord of mind and purpose, the only real social bond. They are the force by which human relations are kept from disintegrating into an aggregate of unconnected and conflicting atoms. His work and that of his followers was a powerful counterpoise to the anti-historic quality of the Benthamite school. The leading scientific interest of the nineteenth century came to be history, including evolution within the scope of history. Coleridge was no historian; he had no great interest in historical facts. But his sense of the mission of great historic institutions was profound. Wordsworth preached the gospel of return to nature, of nature expressed in rivers, dales and mountains and in the souls of simple folk. Implicitly and often explicitly he attacked industrialization as the great foe of nature, without and within. Carlyle carried on a constant battle against utilitarianism and the existing socio-economic order, which he summed up in a single phrase as "anarchy plus a constable." He called for a régime of social authority to enforce social ties. Ruskin preached the social importance of art and joined to it a denunciation of the entire reigning system of economics, theoretical and practical. The esthetic socialists of the school of William Morris carried his teachings home to the popular mind.

The romantic movement profoundly affected some who had grown up in the straitest sect of *laissez faire* liberalism. The intellectual career of John Stuart Mill was a valiant if unsuccessful struggle to reconcile the doctrines he derived, almost in infancy, from his father with a feeling of their hollowness when compared with the values of poetry, of enduring historic institutions, and of the inner life, as portrayed by the romanticists. He was keenly sensitive to the brutality of life about him and its low intellectual level, and saw the relation between these two traits. At one time, he even went so far as to say that he looked forward to the coming of an age "when the division of the produce of labour . . . will be made by concert on an acknowledged principle of justice." He asserted that existing institutions were merely provisional, and that the "laws" governing the distribution of wealth are not social but of man's contrivance and are man's to change. A long distance lies between the philosophy embodied in such sayings and his earlier assertion that "the sole end for which mankind are warranted, individually or collectively, in interfering with the freedom of action of any person is self-protection." The romantic school was the chief influence in effecting the change.

There was in addition another intellectual force at work in changing the earlier liberalism, which openly professed liberal aims while at the same time attacking earlier liberalism. The name of Thomas Hill Green is not widely known outside of technical philosophical circles. But he was the leader in introducing into England, in coherent formulation, the organic idealism that originated in Germany—and that originated there largely in reaction against the basic philosophy of individualistic liberalism and individualistic empiricism. John Mill himself was greatly troubled by the consequences that followed from the psychological doctrine of associationalism. Mental bonds in belief and purpose which are the product of external associations can easily be broken when circumstances change. The moral and social consequence is a threatened destruction of all stable bases of belief and social relationship. Green and his followers exposed this weakness in all phases of the atomistic philosophy that had developed under the alleged empiricism of the earlier liberal school. They criticized piece by piece almost every item of the theory of mind, knowledge and society that had grown out of the teachings of Locke. They asserted that *relations* constitute the reality of nature, of mind and of society. But Green and his followers remained faithful, as the romantic school did not, to the ideals of liberalism; the conceptions of a common good as the measure of political organization and policy, of liberty as the most precious trait and very seal of individuality, of the claim of every individual to the full development of his capacities. They strove to provide unshakeable objective foundations in the very structure of things for these moral claims, instead of basing them upon the sandy ground of the feelings of isolated human beings. For the relations that constitute the essential nature of things are, according to them, the expression of an objective Reason and Spirit that sustains nature and the human mind.

The idealistic philosophy taught that men are held together by the relations that proceed from and that manifest an ultimate cosmic mind. It followed that the basis of society and the state is shared intelligence and purpose, not force nor yet self-interest. The state is a moral organism, of which government is one organ. Only by participating in the common intelligence and sharing in the common purpose as it works for the common good can individual human beings realize their true individualities and become truly free. The state is but one organ among many of the Spirit and Will that holds all things together and that makes human beings members of one another. It does not originate the moral claim of individuals to the full realization of their potentialities as vehicles of objective thought and purpose. Moreover, the motives it can directly appeal to are not of the highest kind. But it is the business of the state to protect all forms and to promote all modes of human association in which the moral claims of the members of society are embodied and which serve as the means of voluntary self-realization. Its business is negatively to remove the obstacles that stand in the way of individuals coming to consciousness of themselves for what they are, and positively to promote the cause of public education. Unless the state does this work it is no state. These philosophical liberals pointed out the restrictions, economic and political, which prevent many, probably the majority, of individuals from the voluntary intelligent action by which they may become what they are capable of becoming. The teachings of this new liberal school affected the thoughts and actions of multitudes who did not trouble themselves to understand the philosophical doctrine that underlay it. They served to break down the idea that freedom is something that individuals have as a ready-made possession, and to instill the idea that it is something to be achieved, while the possibility of the achievement was shown to be conditioned by the institutional medium in which an individual lives. These new liberals fostered the idea that the state has the responsibility for creating institutions under which individuals can effectively realize the potentialities that are theirs.

Thus from various sources and under various influences there developed an inner split in liberalism. This cleft is one cause of the ambiguity from which liberalism still suffers and which explains a growing impotency. There are still those who call themselves liberals who define liberalism in terms of the old opposition between the province of organized social action and the province of purely individual initiative and effort. In the name of liberalism they are jealous of every extension of governmental activity. They may grudgingly concede the need of special measures of protection and alleviation undertaken by the state at times of great social stress, but they are the confirmed enemies of social legislation (even prohibition of child labor), as standing measures of political policy. Wittingly or unwittingly, they still provide the intellectual system of apologetics for the existing economic régime, which they strangely, it would seem ironically, uphold as a régime of individual liberty for all.

But the majority who call themselves liberals today are committed to the principle that organized society must use its powers to establish the conditions under which the mass of individuals can possess actual as distinct from merely legal liberty. They define their liberalism in the concrete in terms of a program of measures moving toward this end. They believe that the conception of the state which limits the activities of the latter to keeping order as between individuals and to securing redress for one person when another person infringes the liberty existing law has given him, is in effect simply a justification of the brutalities and inequities of the existing order.

Because of this internal division within liberalism its later history is wavering and confused. The inheritance of the past still causes many liberals, who believe in a generous use of the powers of organized society to change the terms on which human beings associate together, to stop short with merely protective and alleviatory measures—a fact that partly explains why another school always refers to "reform" with ᵣ ᵤorn. It will be the object of the next chapter to portray the crisis in liberalism, the *impasse* in which it now almost finds itself, and through criticism of the deficiencies of earlier liberalism to suggest the way in which liberalism may resolve the crisis, and emerge as a compact, aggressive force.

2. THE CRISIS IN LIBERALISM

The net effect of the struggle of early liberals to emancipate individuals from restrictions imposed upon them by the inherited type of social organization was to pose a problem, that of a new social organization. The ideas of liberals set forth in the first third of the nineteenth century were potent in criticism and in analysis. They released forces that had been held in check. But analysis is not construction, and release of force does not of itself give direction to the force that is set free. Victorian optimism concealed for a time the crisis at which liberalism had arrived. But when that optimism vanished amid the conflict of nations, classes and races characteristic of the latter part of the nineteenth century—a conflict that has grown more intense with the passing years—the crisis could no longer be covered up. The beliefs and methods of earlier liberalism were ineffective when faced with the problems of social organization and integration. Their inadequacy is a large part of belief now so current that all liberalism is an outmoded doctrine. At the same time, insecurity and uncertainty in belief and purpose

are powerful factors in generating dogmatic faiths that are profoundly hostile to everything to which liberalism in any possible formulation is devoted.

In a longer treatment, the crisis could be depicted in terms
of the career of John Stuart Mill, during a period when the full
force of the crisis was not yet clearly manifest. He records in his
Autobiography that, as early as 1826, he asked himself this question: "Suppose that all your objects in life were realized: that all
the changes in institutions and opinions which you are looking
forward to, could be completely effected at this very instant:
would this be a great joy and happiness to you?" His answer was
negative. The struggle for liberation had given him the satisfaction that comes from active struggle. But the prospect of the
goal attained presented him with a scene in which something
unqualifiedly necessary for the good life was lacking. He found
something profoundly empty in the spectacle he imaginatively
faced. Doubtless physical causes had something to do with his
growing doubt as to whether life would be worth living were
the goal of his ambitious realized; sensitive youth often under-
goes such crises. But he also felt that there was something
inherently superficial in the philosophy of Bentham and his
father. This philosophy now seemed to him to touch only the
externals of life, but not its inner springs of personal suste-
nance and growth. I think it a fair paraphrase to say that he
found himself faced with only intellectual abstractions. Criticism has made us familiar with the abstraction known as the
economic man. The utilitarians added the abstraction of the
legal and political man. But somehow they had failed to touch
man himself. Mill first found relief in the fine arts, especially
poetry, as a medium for the cultivation of the feelings, and
reacted against Benthamism as exclusively intellectualistic, a

theory that identified man with a reckoning machine. Then under the influence of Coleridge and his disciples he learned that institutions and traditions are indispensable to the nurture of what is deepest and most worthy in human life. Acquaintance with Comte's philosophy of a future society based on the organization of science gave him a new end for which to strive, the institution of a kind of social organization in which there should be some central spiritual authority.

The life-long struggle of Mill to reconcile these ideas with those which were deeply graven in his being by his earlier Benthamism concern us here only as a symbol of the enduring crisis of belief and action brought about in liberalism itself when the need arose for uniting earlier ideas of freedom with an insistent demand for social organization, that is, for constructive synthesis in the realm of thought and social institutions. The problem of achieving freedom was immeasurably widened and deepened. It did not now present itself as a conflict between government and the liberty of individuals in matters of conscience and economic action, but as a problem of establishing an entire social order, possessed of a spiritual authority that would nurture and direct the inner as well as the outer life of individuals. The problem of science was no longer merely technological applications for increase of material productivity, but imbuing the minds of individuals with the spirit of reasonableness, fostered by social organization and contributing to its development. The problem of democracy was seen to be not solved, hardly more than externally touched, by the establishment of universal suffrage and representative government. As Havelock Ellis has said, "We see now that the vote and the ballot-box do not make the voter free from even external pressure; and, which is of much more consequence, they do not necessarily free him from his own slavish instincts." The problem of democracy becomes the problem of that form of social organization, extending to all the areas and ways of living, in which the powers of individuals shall not be merely released from mechanical external constraint but shall be fed, sustained and directed. Such an organization demands much more of education than general schooling, which without a renewal of the springs of purpose and desire becomes a new mode of mechanization and formalization, as hostile to liberty as ever was governmental constraint. It demands of science much more than external technical application—which again leads to mechanization of life and results in a new kind of enslavement. It demands that the method of inquiry, of discrimination, of test by verifiable consequences, be naturalized in all the matters, of large and of detailed scope, that arise for judgment.

The demand for a form of social organization that should include economic activities but yet should convert them into servants of the development of the higher capacities of individuals, is one that earlier liberalism did not meet. If we strip its creed from adventitious elements, there are, however, enduring values for which earlier liberalism stood. These values are liberty, the development of the inherent capacities of individuals made possible through liberty, and the central role of free intelligence in inquiry, discussion and expression. But elements that were adventitious to these values colored every one of these ideals in ways that rendered them either impotent or perverse when the new problem of social organization arose.

Before considering the three values, it is advisable to note one adventitious idea that played a large role in the later incapacitation of liberalism. The earlier liberals lacked historic sense and interest. For a while this lack had an immediate pragmatic value. It gave liberals a powerful weapon in their fight with reactionaries. For it enabled them to undercut the appeal to origin, precedent and past history by which the opponents of social change gave sacrosanct quality to existing inequities and abuses. But disregard of history took its revenge. It blinded the eyes of liberals to the fact that their own special interpretations of liberty, individuality and intelligence were themselves historically conditioned, and were relevant only to their own time. They put forward their ideas as immutable truths good at all times and places; they had no idea of historic relativity, either in general or in its application to themselves.

When their ideas and plans were projected they were an attack upon the interests that were vested in established institutions and that had the sanction of custom. The new forces for which liberals sought an entrance were incipient; the *status quo* was arrayed against their release. By the middle of the nineteenth century the contemporary scene had radically altered. The economic and political changes for which they strove were so largely accomplished that they had become in turn the vested interest, and their doctrines, especially in the form of *laissez faire* liberalism, now provided the intellectual justification of the *status quo*. This creed is still powerful in this country. The earlier doctrine of "natural rights," superior to legislative action, has been given a definitely economic meaning by the courts, and used by judges to destroy social legislation passed in the interest of a real, instead of purely formal, liberty of contract. Under the caption of "rugged individualism" it inveighs against all new social policies. Beneficiaries of the established economic régime band themselves together in what they call Liberty Leagues to perpetuate the harsh regimentation of millions of their fellows. I do not imply that resistance to change would not have appeared if it had not been for the doctrines of earlier liberals. But had the early liberals appreciated the historic relativity of their own interpretation of the meaning of liberty, the later resistance would certainly have been deprived of its chief intellectual and moral support. The tragedy is that although these liberals were the sworn foes of political absolutism, they were themselves absolutists in the social creed they formulated.

This statement does not mean, of course, that they were opposed to social change; the opposite is evidently the case. But it does mean they held that beneficial social change can come about in but one way, the way of private economic enterprise, socially undirected, based upon and resulting in the sanctity of private property—that is to say, freedom from social control. So today those who profess the earlier type of liberalism ascribe to this factor all social betterment that has occurred; such as the increase in productivity and improved standards of living. The liberals did not try to prevent change, but they did try to limit its course to a single channel and to immobilize the channel.

If the early liberals had put forth their special interpretation of liberty as something subject to historic relativity they would not have frozen it into a doctrine to be applied at all times under all social circumstances. Specifically, they would have recognized that effective liberty is a function of the social conditions existing at any time. If they had done this, they would have known that as economic relations became dominantly controlling forces in setting the pattern of human relations, the necessity of liberty for individuals which they proclaimed will require social control of economic forces in the interest of the great mass of individuals. Because the liberals failed to make a distinction between purely formal or legal liberty and effective liberty of thought and action, the history of the last one hundred years is the history of non-fulfillment of their predictions. It was prophesied that a régime of economic liberty would bring about interdependence among nations and consequently peace. The actual scene has been marked by wars of increasing scope and destructiveness. Even Karl Marx shared the idea that the new economic forces would destroy economic nationalism and usher in an era of internationalism. The display of exacerbated nationalism now characterizing the world is a sufficient comment. Struggle for raw materials and markets in backward countries, combined with foreign financial control of their domestic industrial development, has been accompanied by all kinds of devices to prevent access of other advanced nations to the national market-place.

The basic doctrine of early economic liberals was that the régime of economic liberty as they conceived it, would almost automatically direct production through competition into channels that would provide, as effectively as possible, socially needed commodities and services. Desire for personal gain early learned that it could better further the satisfaction of that desire by stifling competition and substituting great combinations of noncompeting capital. The liberals supposed the motive of individual self-interest would so release productive energies as to produce ever-increasing abundance. They overlooked the fact that in many cases personal profit can be better served by maintaining artificial scarcity and by what Veblen called systematic sabotage of production. Above all, in identifying the extension of liberty in all of its modes with extension of their particular brand of economic liberty, they completely failed to anticipate the bearing of private control of the means of production and distribution upon the effective liberty of the masses in industry as well as in cultural goods. An era of power possessed by the few took the place of the era of liberty for all envisaged by the liberals of the early nineteenth century.

These statements do not imply that these liberals should or could have foreseen the changes that would occur, due to the impact of new forces of production. The point is that their failure to grasp the historic position of the interpretation of liberty they put forth served later to solidify a social régime that was a chief obstacle to attainment of the ends they professed. One aspect of this failure is worth especial mention. No one has ever seen more clearly than the Benthamites that the political self-interest of rulers, if not socially checked and controlled, leads to actions that destroy liberty for the mass of people. Their perception of this fact was a chief ground for their advocacy of representative government, for they saw in this measure a means by which the self-interest of the rulers would be forced into conformity with the interests of their subjects. But they had no glimpse of the fact that private control of the new forces of production, forces which affect the life of every one, would operate in the same way as private unchecked control of political power. They saw the need of new legal institutions, and of different political conditions as a means to political liberty. But they failed to perceive that social control of economic forces is equally necessary if anything approaching economic equality and liberty is to be realized.

Bentham did believe that increasing equalization of economic fortunes was desirable. He justified his opinion of its desirability on the ground of the greater happiness of the greater number: to put the matter crudely, the possession of ten thousand dollars by a thousand persons would generate a greater sum of happiness than the possession of ten million dollars by one person. But he believed that the régime of economic liberty would of itself tend in the direction of greater equalization. Meantime, he held that "time is the only mediator," and he opposed the use of organized social power to promote equalization on the ground that such action would disturb the "security" that is even a greater condition of happiness than is equality.

When it became evident that disparity, not equality, was the actual consequence of *laissez faire* liberalism, defenders of the latter developed a double system of justifying apologetics. Upon one front, they fell back upon the natural inequalities of individuals in psychological and moral make-up, asserting that inequality of fortune and economic status is the "natural" and justifiable consequence of the free play of these inherent differences. Herbert Spencer even erected this idea into a principle of cosmic justice, based upon the idea of the proportionate relation existing between cause and effect. I fancy that today there are but few who are hardy enough, even admitting the principle of natural inequalities, to assert that the disparities of property and income bear any commensurate ratio to inequalities in the native constitution of individuals. If we suppose that there is in fact such a ratio, the consequences are so intolerable that the practical inference to be drawn is that organized social effort should intervene to prevent the alleged natural law from taking full effect.

The other line of defense is unceasing glorification of the virtues of initiative, independence, choice and responsibility, virtues that centre in and proceed from individuals as such. I am one who believes that we need more, not fewer, "rugged individuals" and it is in the name of rugged individualism that I challenge the argument. Instead of independence, there exists parasitical dependence on a wide scale—witness the present need for the exercise of charity, private and public, on a vast scale. The current argument against the public dole on the ground that it pauperizes and demoralizes those who receive it has an ironical sound when it comes from those who would leave intact the conditions that cause the necessity for recourse to the method of support of millions at public expense. Servility and regimentation are the result of control by the few of access to means of productive labor on the part of the many. An even more serious objection to the argument is that it conceives of initiative, vigor, independence exclusively in terms of their least significant manifestation. They are limited to exercise in the economic area. The meaning of their exercise in connection with the cultural resources of civilization, in such matters as companionship, science and art, is all but ignored. It is at this last point in particular that the crisis of liberalism and the need for a reconsideration of it in terms of the genuine liberation of individuals are most evident. The enormous exaggeration of material and materialistic economics that now prevails at the expense of cultural values, is not itself the result of earlier liberalism. But, as was illustrated in the personal crisis through which Mill passed, it is an exaggeration which is favored, both intellectually and morally, by fixation of the early creed.

This fact induces a natural transition from the concept of liberty to that of the individual. The underlying philosophy and psychology of earlier liberalism led to a conception of individuality as something ready-made, already possessed, and needing only the removal of certain legal restrictions to come into full play. It was not conceived as a moving thing, something that is attained only by continuous growth. Because of this failure, the dependence in fact of individuals upon social conditions was made little of. It is true that some of the early liberals, like John Stuart Mill, made much of the effect of "circumstances" in producing differences among individuals. But the use of the word and idea of "circumstances" is significant. It suggests—and the context bears out the suggestion—that social arrangements and institutions were thought of as things that operate from without, not entering in any significant way into the internal make-up and growth of individuals. Social arrangements were treated not as positive forces but as external limitations. Some passages in Mill's discussion of the logic of the social sciences are pertinent. "Men in a state of society are still men; their actions and passions are obedient to the laws of individual human nature. Men are not, when brought together, converted into a different kind of substance, as hydrogen and oxygen differ from water. . . Human beings in society have no properties but those which are derived from, and may be resolved into, the laws of individual men." And again he says: "The actions and feelings of men in the social state are entirely governed by psychological laws."[1]

There is an implication in these passages that liberals will be the last to deny. This implication is directly in line with Mill's own revolt against the creed in which he was educated. As far as the statements are a warning against attaching undue importance to merely external institutional changes, to changes that do not enter into the desires, purposes and beliefs of the very constitution of individuals, they express an idea to which liberalism is committed by its own nature. But Mill means something at once less and more than this. While he would probably have

---

1. The quotations are from Mill's *Logic*, Book VI, chs. vii and ix.

denied that he held to the notion of a state of nature in which
individuals exist prior to entering into a social state, he is in fact
giving a psychological version of that doctrine. Individuals, it is
implied, have a full-blown psychological and moral nature, having its own set laws, independently of their association with one
another. It is the psychological laws of this isolated human nature
from which social laws are derived and into which they may be
resolved. His own illustration of water in its difference from
hydrogen and oxygen on separation might have taught him better, if it had not been for the influence of a prior dogma. That the
human infant is modified in mind and character by his connection with others in family life and that the modification continues throughout life as his connections with others broaden, is as
true as that hydrogen is modified when it combines with oxygen.
If we generalize the meaning of this fact, it is evident that while
there are native organic or biological structures that remain fairly
constant, the actual "laws" of human nature are laws of individuals in association, not of beings in a mythical condition apart
from association. In other words, liberalism that takes its profession of the importance of individuality with sincerity must be
deeply concerned about the structure of human association. For
the latter operates to affect negatively and positively, the development of individuals. Because a wholly unjustified idea of opposition between individuals and society has become current, and
because its currency has been furthered by the underlying philosophy of individualistic liberalism, there are many who in fact
are working for social changes such that rugged individuals may
exist in reality, that have become contemptuous of the very idea
of individuality, while others support in the name of individualism institutions that militate powerfully against the emergence
and growth of beings possessed of genuine individuality.

It remains to say something of the third enduring value in the liberal creed:—intelligence. Grateful recognition is due early liberals for their valiant battle in behalf of freedom of thought, conscience, expression and communication. The civil liberties we possess, however precariously today, are in large measure the fruit of their efforts and those of the French liberals who engaged in the same battle. But their basic theory as to the nature of intelligence is such as to offer no sure foundation for the permanent victory of the cause they espoused. They resolved mind into a complex of external associations among atomic elements, just as they resolved society itself into a similar compound of external associations among individuals, each of whom has his own independently fixed nature. Their psychology was not in fact the product of impartial inquiry into human nature. It was rather a political weapon devised in the interest of breaking down the rigidity of dogmas and of institutions that had lost their relevancy. Mill's own contention that psychological laws of the kind he laid down were prior to the laws of men living and communicating together, acting and reacting upon one another, was itself a political instrument forged in the interest of criticism of beliefs and institutions that he believed should be displaced. The doctrine was potent in exposure of abuses; it was weak for constructive purposes. Bentham's assertion that he introduced the method of experiment into the social sciences held good as far as resolution into atoms acting externally upon one another, after the Newtonian model, was concerned. It did not recognize the place in experiment of comprehensive social ideas as working hypotheses in direction of action.

The practical consequence was also the logical one. When conditions had changed and the problem was one of constructing social organization from individual units that had been released from old social ties, liberalism fell upon evil times. The conception of intelligence as something that arose from the association of isolated elements, sensations and feelings, left no room for far-reaching experiments in construction of a new social order. It was definitely hostile to everything like collective social planning. The doctrine of *laissez faire* was applied to intelligence as well as to economic action, although the conception of experimental method in science demands a control by comprehensive ideas, projected in possibilities to be realized by action. Scientific method is as much opposed to go-as-you-please in intellectual matters as it is to reliance upon habits of mind whose sanction is that they were formed by "experience" in the past. The theory of mind held by the early liberals advanced beyond dependence upon the past but it did not arrive at the idea of experimental and constructive intelligence.

The dissolving atomistic individualism of the liberal school evoked by way of reaction the theory of organic objective mind. But the effect of the latter theory embodied in idealistic metaphysics was also hostile to intentional social planning. The historical march of mind, embodied in institutions, was believed to account for social changes—all in its own good time. A similar conception was fortified by the interest in history and in evolution so characteristic of the later nineteenth century. The materialistic philosophy of Spencer joined hands with the idealistic doctrine of Hegel in throwing the burden of social direction upon powers that are beyond deliberate social foresight and planning. The economic dialectic of history, substituted by Marx for the Hegelian dialectic of ideas, as interpreted by the social-democratic party in Europe, was taken to signify an equally inevitable movement toward a predestined goal. Moreover, the idealistic theory of objective spirit provided an intellectual justification for the nationalisms that were rising. Concrete manifestation of absolute mind was said to be provided through national states. Today, this philosophy is readily turned to the support of the totalitarian state.

The crisis in liberalism is connected with failure to develop and lay hold of an adequate conception of intelligence integrated with social movements and a factor in giving them direction. We cannot mete out harsh blame to the early liberals for failure to attain such a conception. The first scientific society for the study of anthropology was founded the year in which Darwin's *Origin of Species* saw the light of day. I cite this particular fact to typify the larger fact that the sciences of society, the controlled study of man in his relationships, are the product of the later nineteenth century. Moreover, these disciplines not only came into being too late to influence the formulation of liberal social theory, but they themselves were so much under the influence of the more advanced physical sciences that it was supposed that their findings were of merely theoretic import. By this statement, I mean that although the conclusions of the social disciplines were about man, they were treated as if they were of the same nature as the conclusions of physical science about remote galaxies of stars. Social and historical inquiry is in fact a part of the social process itself, not something outside of it. The consequence of not perceiving this fact was that the conclusions of the social sciences were not made (and still are not made in any large measure) integral members of a program of social action. When the conclusions of inquiries that deal with man are left outside the program of social action, social policies are necessarily left without the guidance that knowledge of man can provide, and that it must provide if social action is not to be directed either by mere precedent and custom or else by the happy intuitions of individual minds. The social conception of the nature and work of intelligence is still miniature; in consequence, its use as a director of social action is inchoate and sporadic. It is the tragedy of earlier liberalism that just at the time when the problem of social organization was most urgent, liberals could bring to its solution nothing but the conception that intelligence is an individual possession.

It is all but a commonplace that today physical knowledge and its technical applications have far outrun our knowledge of man and its application in social invention and engineering. What I have just said indicates a deep source of the trouble. After all, our accumulated knowledge of man and his ways, furnished by anthropology, history, sociology and psychology, is vast, even though it be sparse in comparison with our knowledge of physical nature. But it is still treated as so much merely theoretic knowledge amassed by specialists, and at most communicated by them in books and articles to the general public. We are habituated to the idea that every discovery in physical knowledge signifies, sooner or later, a change in the processes of production; there are countless persons whose business it is to see that these discoveries take effect through invention in improved operations in practice. There is next to nothing of the same sort with respect to knowledge of man and human affairs. Although the latter is recognized to concern man in the sense of being *about* him, it is of less practical effect than are the much more remote findings of physical science.

The inchoate state of social knowledge is reflected in the

two fields where intelligence might be supposed to be most alert and most continuously active, education and the formation of social policies in legislation. Science is taught in our schools. But very largely it appears in schools simply as another study, to be acquired by much the same methods as are employed in "learning" the older studies that are part of the curriculum. If it were treated as what it is, the method of intelligence itself in action, then the method of science would be incarnate in every branch of study and every detail of learning. Thought would be connected with the possibility of action, and every mode of action would be reviewed to see its bearing upon the habits and ideas from which it sprang. Until science is treated educationally in this way, the introduction of what is called science into the schools signifies one more opportunity for the mechanization of the material and methods of study. When "learning" is treated not as an expansion of the understanding and judgment of meanings but as an acquisition of information, the method of cooperative experimental intelligence finds its way into the working structure of the individual only incidentally and by devious paths.

Of the place and use of socially organized intelligence in the conduct of public affairs, through legislation and administration, I shall have something to say in the next chapter. At this point of the discussion I am content to ask the reader to compare the force it now exerts in politics with that of the interest of individuals and parties in capturing and retaining office and power, with that exercised by the propaganda of publicity agents and that of organized pressure groups.

Humanly speaking, the crisis in liberalism was a product of particular historical events. Soon after liberal tenets were formulated as eternal truths, it became an instrument of vested

54

interests in opposition to further social change, a ritual of lip-service, or else was shattered by new forces that came in. Nev-ertheless, the ideas of liberty, of individuality and of freed intel-ligence have an enduring value, a value never more needed than now. It is the business of liberalism to state these values in ways, intellectual and practical, that are relevant to present needs and forces. If we employ the conception of historic rela-tivity, nothing is clearer than that the conception of liberty is always relative to forces that at a given time and place are increasingly felt to be oppressive. Liberty in the concrete sig-nifies release from the impact of particular oppressive forces; emancipation from something once taken as a normal part of human life but now experienced as bondage. At one time, lib-erty signified liberation from chattel slavery; at another time, release of a class from serfdom. During the late seventeenth and early eighteenth centuries it meant liberation from despotic dynastic rule. A century later it meant release of industrialists from inherited legal customs that hampered the rise of new forces of production. Today, it signifies liberation from mater-ial insecurity and from the coercions and repressions that pre-vent multitudes from participation in the vast cultural resources that are at hand. The direct impact of liberty always has to do with some class or group that is suffering in a special way from some form of constraint exercised by the distribution of powers that exists in contemporary society. Should a class-less society ever come into being the formal *concept* of liberty would lose its significance, because the *fact* for which it stands would have become an integral part of the established relations of human beings to one another.

Until such a time arrives liberalism will continue to have a necessary social office to perform. Its task is the mediation of social transitions. This phrase may seem to some to be a virtual admission that liberalism is a colorless "middle of the road" doctrine. Not so, even though liberalism has sometimes taken that form in practice. We are always dependent upon the experience that has accumulated in the past and yet there are always new forces coming in, new needs arising, that demand, if the new forces are to operate and the new needs to be satisfied, a reconstruction of the patterns of old experience. The old and the new have forever to be integrated with each other, so that the values of old experience may become the servants and instruments of new desires and aims. We are always possessed by habits and customs, and this fact signifies that we are always influenced by the inertia and the momentum of forces temporally outgrown but nevertheless still present with us as a part of our being. Human life gets set in patterns, institutional and moral. But change is also with us and demands the constant remaking of old habits and old ways of thinking, desiring and acting. The effective ratio between the old and the stabilizing and the new and disturbing is very different at different times. Sometimes whole communities seem to be dominated by custom, and changes are produced only by irruptions and invasions from outside. Sometimes, as at present, change is so varied and accelerated that customs seem to be dissolving before our very eyes. But be the ratio little or great, there is always an adjustment to be made, and as soon as the need for it becomes conscious, liberalism has a function and a meaning. It is not that liberalism creates the need, but that the necessity for adjustment defines the office of liberalism.

For the only adjustment that does not have to be made over again, and perhaps even under more unfavorable circumstances than when it was first attempted, is that effected

56

through intelligence as a method. In its large sense, this remaking of the old through union with the new is precisely what intelligence is. It is conversion of past experience into knowledge and projection of that knowledge in ideas and purposes that anticipate what may come to be in the future and that indicate how to realize what is desired. Every problem that arises, personal or collective, simple or complex, is solved only by selecting material from the store of knowledge amassed in past experience and by bringing into play habits already formed. But the knowledge and the habits have to be modified to meet the new conditions that have arisen. In collective problems, the habits that are involved are traditions and institutions. The standing danger is either that they will be acted upon implicitly, without reconstruction to meet new conditions, or else that there will be an impatient and blind rush forward, directed only by some dogma rigidly adhered to. The office of intelligence in every problem that either a person or a community meets is to effect a working connection between old habits, customs, institutions, beliefs, and new conditions. What I have called the mediating function of liberalism is all one with the work of intelligence. This fact is the root, whether it be consciously realized or not, of the emphasis placed by liberalism upon the role of freed intelligence as the method of directing social action.

Objections that are brought against liberalism ignore the fact that the only alternatives to dependence upon intelligence are either drift and casual improvisation, or the use of coercive force stimulated by unintelligent emotion and fanatical dogmatism—the latter being intolerant by its very constitution. The objection that the method of intelligence has been tried and failed is wholly aside from the point, since the crux of the present situation is that it has not been tried under such conditions as now exist. It has not been tried at any time with use of all the resources that scientific material and the experimental method now put at our disposal. It is also said that intelligence is cold and that persons are moved to new ways of acting only by emotion, just as habit makes them adhere to old ways. Of course, intelligence does not generate action except as it is enkindled by feeling. But the notion that there is some inherent opposition between emotion and intelligence is a relic of the notion of mind that grew up before the experimental method of science had emerged. For the latter method signifies the union of ideas with action, a union that is intimate; and action generates and supports emotion. Ideas that are framed to be put into operation for the sake of guiding action are imbued with all the emotional force that attaches to the ends proposed for action, and are accompanied with all the excitement and inspiration that attends the struggle to realize the ends. Since the ends of liberalism are liberty and the opportunity of individuals to secure full realization of their potentialities, all of the emotional intensity that belongs to these ends gathers about the ideas and acts that are necessary to make them real.

Again, it is said that the average citizen is not endowed with the degree of intelligence that the use of it as a method demands. This objection, supported by alleged scientific findings about heredity and by impressive statistics concerning the intelligence quotient of the average citizen, rests wholly upon the old notion that intelligence is a ready-made possession of individuals. The last stand of oligarchical and anti-social seclusion is perpetuation of this purely individualistic notion of intelligence. The reliance of liberalism is not upon the mere abstraction of a native endowment unaffected by social relationships, but upon the fact that native capacity is sufficient to enable the average individual to respond to and to use the knowledge and the skill that are embodied in the social conditions in which he lives, moves and has his being. There are few individuals who have the native capacity that was required to invent the stationary steam-engine, locomotive, dynamo or telephone. But there are none so mean that they cannot intelligently utilize these embodiments of intelligence once they are a part of the organized means of associated living.

The indictments that are drawn against the intelligence of individuals are in truth indictments of a social order that does not permit the average individual to have access to the rich store of the accumulated wealth of mankind in knowledge, ideas and purposes. There does not now exist the kind of social organization that even permits the average human being to share the potentially available social intelligence. Still less is there a social order that has for one of its chief purposes the establishment of conditions that will move the mass of individuals to appropriate and use what is at hand. Back of the appropriation by the few of the material resources of society lies the appropriation by the few in behalf of their own ends of the cultural, the spiritual, resources that are the product not of the individuals who have taken possession but of the cooperative work of humanity. It is useless to talk about the failure of democracy until the source of its failure has been grasped and steps are taken to bring about that type of social organization that will encourage the socialized extension of intelligence.

The crisis in liberalism, as I said at the outset, proceeds from the fact that after early liberalism had done its work, society faced a new problem, that of social organization. Its work was to liberate a group of individuals, representing the new science and the new forces of productivity, from customs, ways of thinking, institutions, that were oppressive of the new modes of social action, however useful they may have been in their day. The instruments of analysis, of criticism, of dissolution, that were employed were effective for the work of release. But when it came to the problem of organizing the new forces and the individuals whose modes of life they radically altered into a coherent social organization, possessed of intellectual and moral directive power, liberalism was well-nigh impotent. The rise of national polities that pretend to represent the order, discipline and spiritual authority that will counteract social disintegration is a tragic comment upon the unpreparedness of older liberalism to deal with the new problem which its very success precipitated.

But the values of freed intelligence, of liberty, of opportunity for every individual to realize the potentialities of which he is possessed, are too precious to be sacrificed to a régime of despotism, especially when the régime is in such large measure merely the agent of a dominant economic class in its struggle to keep and extend the gains it has amassed at the expense of genuine social order, unity, and development. Liberalism has to gather itself together to formulate the ends to which it is devoted in terms of means that are relevant to the contemporary situation. The only form of enduring social organization that is now possible is one in which the new forces of productivity are cooperatively controlled and used in the interest of the effective liberty and the cultural development of the individuals that constitute society. Such a social order cannot be established by an unplanned and external convergence of the actions of separate individuals, each of whom is bent on personal private advantage. This idea is the Achilles heel of early liberalism. The idea that liberalism cannot maintain its ends and at the same time reverse its conception of the means by which they are to be attained is folly. The ends can now be achieved *only* by reversal of the means to which early liberalism was committed. Organized social planning, put into effect for the creation of an order in which industry and finance are socially directed in behalf of institutions that provide the material basis for the cultural liberation and growth of individuals, is now the sole method of social action by which liberalism can realize its professed alms. Such planning demands in turn a new conception and logic of freed intelligence as a social force. To these phases of a renascent liberalism, I turn in the chapter that follows.

3. RENASCENT LIBERALISM

Nothing is blinder than the supposition that we live in a society and world so static that either nothing new will happen or else it will happen because of the use of violence. Social change is here as a fact, a fact having multifarious forms and marked in intensity. Changes that are revolutionary in effect are in process in every phase of life. Transformations in the family, the church, the school, in science and art, in economic and political relations, are occurring so swiftly that imagination is baffled in attempt to lay hold of them. Flux does not have to be created. But it does have to be directed. It has to be so controlled that it will move to some end in accordance with the principles of life, since life itself is development. Liberalism is committed to an end that is at once enduring and flexible: the liberation of individuals so that realization of their capacities may be the law of their life. It is committed to the use of freed intelligence as the method of directing change. In any case, civilization is faced with the problem of uniting the changes that are going on into a coherent pattern of social organization.

61

The liberal spirit is marked by its own picture of the pattern that is required: a social organization that will make possible effective liberty and opportunity for personal growth in mind and spirit in all individuals. Its present need is recognition that established material security is a prerequisite of the ends which it cherishes, so that, the basis of life being secure, individuals may actively share in the wealth of cultural resources that now exist and may contribute, each in his own way, to their further enrichment.

The fact of change has been so continual and so intense that it overwhelms our minds. We are bewildered by the spectacle of its rapidity, scope and intensity. It is not surprising that men have protected themselves from the impact of such vast change by resorting to what psycho-analysis has taught us to call rationalizations, in other words, protective fantasies. The Victorian idea that change is a part of an evolution that necessarily leads through successive stages to some preordained divine far-off event is one rationalization. The conception of a sudden, complete, almost catastrophic, transformation, to be brought about by the victory of the proletariat over the class now dominant, is a similar rationalization. But men have met the impact of change in the realm of actuality, mostly by drift and by temporary, usually incoherent, improvisations. Liberalism, like every other theory of life, has suffered from the state of confused uncertainty that is the lot of a world suffering from rapid and varied change for which there is no intellectual and moral preparation.

Because of this lack of mental and moral preparation the impact of swiftly moving changes produced, as I have just said, confusion, uncertainty and drift. Change in patterns of belief, desire and purpose has lagged behind the modification of the external conditions under which men associate. Industrial habits have changed most rapidly; there has followed considerable distance, change in political relations; alterations in legal relations and methods have lagged even more, while changes in the institutions that deal most directly with patterns of thought and belief have taken place to the least extent. This fact defines the primary, though not by any means the ultimate, responsibility of a liberalism that intends to be a vital force. Its work is first of all education, in the broadest sense of that term. Schooling is a part of the work of education, but education in its full meaning includes all the influences that go to form the attitudes and dispositions (of desire as well as of belief), which constitute dominant habits of mind and character.

Let me mention three changes that have taken place in one of the institutions in which immense shifts have occurred, but that are still relatively external—external in the sense that the pattern of intelligent purpose and emotion has not been correspondingly modified. Civilization existed for most of human history in a state of scarcity in the material basis for a humane life. Our ways of thinking, planning and working have been attuned to this fact. Thanks to science and technology we now live in an age of potential plenty. The immediate effect of the emergence of the new possibility was simply to stimulate, to a point of incredible exaggeration, the striving for the material resources, called wealth, opened to men in the new vista. It is a characteristic of all development, physiological and mental, that when a new force and factor appears, it is first pushed to an extreme. Only when its possibilities have been exhausted (at least relatively) does it take its place in the life perspective. The economic-material phase of life, which belongs in the basal ganglia of society, has usurped for more than a century the cortex of the social body. The habits of desire and effort that were bred in the age of scarcity do not readily subordinate themselves and take the place of the matter-of-course routine that becomes appropriate to them when machines and impersonal power have the capacity to liberate man from bondage to the strivings that were once needed to make secure his physical basis. Even now when there is a vision of an age of abundance and when the vision is supported by hard fact, it is material security as an end that appeals to most rather than the way of living which this security makes possible. Men's minds are still pathetically held in the clutch of old habits and haunted by old memories.

For, in the second place, insecurity is the natural child and the foster child, too, of scarcity. Early liberalism emphasized the importance of insecurity as a fundamentally necessary economic motive, holding that without this goad men would not work, abstain or accumulate. Formulation of this conception was new. But the fact that was formulated was nothing new. It was deeply rooted in the habits that were formed in the long struggle against material scarcity. The system that goes by the name of capitalism is a systematic manifestation of desires and purposes built up in an age of ever threatening want and now carried over into a time of ever increasing potential plenty. The conditions that generate insecurity for the many no longer spring from nature. They are found in institutions and arrangements that are within deliberate human control. Surely this change marks one of the greatest revolutions that has taken place in all human history. Because of it, insecurity is not now the motive to work and sacrifice but to despair. It is not an instigation to put forth energy but to an impotency that can be converted from death into endurance only by charity. But the habits of mind and action that modify institutions to make potential abundance an actuality are still so inchoate that most of us discuss labels like individualism, socialism and communism instead of even perceiving the possibility, much less the necessity for realizing what can and should be.

In the third place, the patterns of belief and purpose that still dominate economic institutions were formed when individuals produced with their hands, alone or in small groups. The notion that society in general is served by the unplanned coincidence of the consequences of a vast multitude of efforts put forth by isolated individuals without reference to any social end, was also something new as a formulation. But it also formulated the working principle of an epoch which the advent of new forces of production was to bring to an end. It demands no great power of intelligence to see that under present conditions the isolated individual is well-nigh helpless. Concentration and corporate organization are the rule. But the concentration and corporate organization are still controlled in their operation by ideas that were institutionalized in eons of separate individual effort. The attempts at cooperation for mutual benefit that are put forth are precious as experimental moves. But that society itself should see to it that a cooperative industrial order be instituted, one that is consonant with the realities of production enforced by an era of machinery and power, is so novel an idea to the general mind that its mere suggestion is hailed with abusive epithets—sometimes with imprisonment.

When, then, I say that the first object of a renascent liberalism is education, I mean that its task is to aid in producing the habits of mind and character, the intellectual and moral patterns, that are somewhere near even with the actual movements of events. It is, I repeat, the split between the latter as they have externally occurred and the ways of desiring, thinking, and of putting emotion and purpose into execution that is the basic cause of present confusion in mind and paralysis in action. The educational task cannot be accomplished merely by working upon men's minds, without action that effects actual change in institutions. The idea that dispositions and attitudes can be altered by merely "moral" means conceived of as something that goes on wholly inside of persons is itself one of the old patterns that has to be changed. Thought, desire and purpose exist in a constant give and take of interaction with environing conditions. But resolute thought is the first step in that change of action that will itself carry further the needed change in patterns of mind and character.

In short, liberalism must now become radical, meaning by "radical" perception of the necessity of thoroughgoing changes in the set-up of institutions and corresponding activity to bring the changes to pass. For the gulf between what the actual situation makes possible and the actual state itself is so great that it cannot be bridged by piecemeal policies undertaken *ad hoc*. The process of producing the changes will be, in any case, a gradual one. But "reforms" that deal now with this abuse and now with that without having a social goal based upon an inclusive plan, differ entirely from effort at re-forming, in its literal sense, the institutional scheme of things. The liberals of more than a century ago were denounced in their time as subversive radicals, and only when the new economic order was established did they become apologists for the *status quo* or else content with social patchwork. If radicalism be defined as perception of need for radical change, then today any liberalism which is not also radicalism is irrelevant and doomed.

But radicalism also means, in the minds of many, both sup-
porters and opponents, dependence upon use of violence as the
main method of effecting drastic changes. Here the liberal
parts company. For he is committed to the organization of
intelligent action as the chief method. Any frank discussion of
the issue must recognize the extent to which those who decry
the use of any violence are themselves willing to resort to violence and are ready to put their will into operation. Their fundamental objection is to change in the economic institution
that now exists, and for its maintenance they resort to the use
of the force that is placed in their hands by this very institution.
They do not need to advocate the use of force; their only need
is to employ it. Force, rather than intelligence, is built into the
procedures of the existing social system, regularly as coercion,
in times of crisis as overt violence. The legal system, conspic-
uously in its penal aspect, more subtly in civil practice, rests
upon coercion. Wars are the methods recurrently used in set-
tlement of disputes between nations. One school of radicals
dwells upon the fact that in the past the transfer of power in
one society has either been accomplished by or attended with
violence. But what we need to realize is that physical force is
used, at least in the form of coercion, in the very set-up of our
society. That the competitive system, which was thought of by
early liberals as the means by which the latent abilities of individuals were to be evoked and directed into socially useful
channels, is now in fact a state of scarcely disguised battle
hardly needs to be dwelt upon. That the control of the means
of production by the few in legal possession operates as a standing agency of coercion of the many, may need emphasis in
statement, but is surely evident to one who is willing to observe
and honestly report the existing scene. It is foolish to regard the

political state as the only agency now endowed with coercive power. Its exercise of this power is pale in contrast with that exercised by concentrated and organized property interests.

It is not surprising in view of our standing dependence upon the use of coercive force that at every time of crisis coercion breaks out into open violence. In this country, with its tradition of violence fostered by frontier conditions and by the conditions under which immigration went on during the greater part of our history, resort to violence is especially recurrent on the part of those who are in power. In times of imminent change, our verbal and sentimental worship of the Constitution, with its guarantees of civil liberties of expression, publication and assemblage, readily goes overboard. Often the officials of the law are the worst offenders, acting as agents of some power that rules the economic life of a community. What is said about the value of free speech as a safety valve is then forgotten with the utmost of ease: a comment, perhaps, upon the weakness of the defense of freedom of expression that values it simply as a means of blowing-off steam.

It is not pleasant to face the extent to which, as matter of fact, coercive and violent force is relied upon in the present social system as a means of social control. It is much more agreeable to evade the fact. But unless the fact is acknowledged as a fact in its full depth and breadth, the meaning of dependence upon intelligence as the alternative method of social direction will not be grasped. Failure in acknowledgment signifies, among other things, failure to realize that those who propagate the dogma of dependence upon force have the sanction of much that is already entrenched in the existing system. They would but turn the use of it to opposite ends. The assumption that the method of intelligence already rules and that those who urge the use of violence are introducing a new element into the social picture may not be hypocritical but it is unintelligently unaware of what is actually involved in intelligence as an alternative method of social action.

I begin with an example of what is really involved in the issue. Why is it, apart from our tradition of violence, that liberty of expression is tolerated and even lauded when social affairs seem to be going in a quiet fashion, and yet is so readily destroyed whenever matters grow critical? The general answer, of course, is that at bottom social institutions have habituated us to the use of force in some veiled form. But a part of the answer is found in our ingrained habit of regarding intelligence as an individual possession and its exercise as an individual right. It is false that freedom of inquiry and of expression are not modes of action. They are exceedingly potent modes of action. The reactionary grasps this fact, in practice if not in express idea, more quickly than the liberal, who is too much given to holding that this freedom is innocent of consequences, as well as being a merely individual right. The result is that this liberty is tolerated as long as it does not seem to menace in any way the *status quo* of society. When it does, every effort is put forth to identify the established order with the public good. When this identification is established, it follows that any merely individual right must yield to the general welfare. As long as freedom of thought and speech is claimed as a merely individual right, it will give way, as do other merely personal claims, when it is, or is successfully represented to be, in opposition to the general welfare.

I would not in the least disparage the noble fight waged by early liberals in behalf of individual freedom of thought and expression. We owe more to them than it is possible to record in words. No more eloquent words have ever come from any one than those of Justice Brandeis in the case of a legislative act that in fact restrained freedom of political expression. He said: "Those who won our independence believed that the final end of the State was to make men free to develop their faculties, and that in its government the deliberative forces should prevail over the arbitrary. They valued liberty both as an end and as a means. They believed liberty to be the secret of happiness and courage to be the secret of liberty. They believed that freedom to think as you will and to speak as you think are means indispensable to the discovery and spread of political truth; that without free speech and assembly discussion would be futile; that with them, discussion affords ordinarily adequate protection against the dissemination of noxious doctrines; that the greatest menace to freedom is ail inert people; that public discussion is a political duty; and that this should be a fundamental principle of the American Government." This is the creed of a fighting liberalism. But the issue I am raising is connected with the fact that these words are found in a dissenting, a minority opinion of the Supreme Court of the United States. The public function of free individual thought and speech is clearly recognized in the words quoted. But the reception of the truth of the words is met by an obstacle: the old habit of defending liberty of thought and expression as something inhering in individuals apart from and even in opposition to social claims.

Liberalism has to assume the responsibility for making it clear that intelligence is a social asset and is clothed with a function as public as is its origin, in the concrete, in social cooperation. It was Comte who, in reaction against the purely individualistic ideas that seemed to him to underlie the French

Revolution, said that in mathematics, physics and astronomy there is no right of private conscience. If we remove the statement from the context of actual scientific procedure, it is dangerous because it is false. The individual inquirer has not only the right but the duty to criticize the ideas, theories and "laws" that are current in science. But if we take the statement in the context of scientific method, it indicates that he carries on this criticism in virtue of a socially generated body of knowledge and by means of methods that are not of private origin and possession. He uses a method that retains public validity even when innovations are introduced in its use and application.

Henry George, speaking of ships that ply the ocean with a velocity of five or six hundred miles a day, remarked, "There is nothing whatever to show that the men who to-day build and navigate and use such ships are one whit superior in any physical or mental quality to their ancestors, whose best vessel was a coracle of wicker and hide. The enormous improvement which these ships show is not an improvement of human nature; it is an improvement of society—it is due to a wider and fuller union of individual efforts in accomplishment of common ends." This single instance, duly pondered, gives a better idea of the nature of intelligence and its social office than would a volume of abstract dissertation. Consider merely two of the factors that enter in and their social consequences. Consider what is involved in the production of steel, from the first use of fire and then the crude smelting of ore, to the processes that now effect the mass production of steel. Consider also the development of the power of guiding ships across trackless wastes from the day when they hugged the shore, steering by visible sun and stars, to the appliances that now enable a sure course to be taken. It would require a heavy tome to describe the advances in science, in mathematics, astronomy, physics, chemistry, that have made these two things possible. The record would be an account of a vast multitude of cooperative efforts, in which one individual uses the results provided for him by a countless number of other individuals, and uses them so as to add to the common and public store. A survey of such facts brings home the actual social character of intelligence as it actually develops and makes its way. Survey of the consequences upon the ways of living of individuals and upon the terms on which men associate together, due to the new method of transportation would take us to the wheat farmer of the prairies, the cattle raiser of the plains, the cotton grower of the South; into a multitude of mills and factories, and to the counting-room of banks, and what would be seen in this country would be repeated in every country of the globe.

It is to such things as these, rather than to abstract and formal psychology that we must go if we would learn the nature of intelligence: in itself, in its origin and development, and its uses and consequences. At this point, I should like to recur to an idea put forward in the preceding chapter. I then referred to the contempt often expressed for reliance upon intelligence as a social method, and I said this scorn is due to the identification of intelligence with native endowments of individuals. In contrast to this notion, I spoke of the power of individuals to appropriate and respond to the intelligence, the knowledge, ideas and purposes that have been integrated in the medium in which individuals live.

Each of us knows, for example, some mechanic of ordinary native capacity who is intelligent within the matters of his calling. He has lived in an environment in which the cumulative intelligence of a multitude of cooperating individuals is embodied, and by the use of his native capacities he makes some phase of this intelligence his own. Given a social medium in whose institutions the available knowledge, ideas and art of humanity were incarnate, and the average individual would rise to undreamed heights of social and political intelligence.

The rub, the problem is found in the proviso. Can the intelligence actually existent and potentially available be embodied in that institutional medium in which an individual thinks, desires and acts? Before dealing directly with this question, I wish to say something about the operation of intelligence in our present political institutions, as exemplified by current practices of democratic government. I would not minimize the advance scored in substitution of methods of discussion and conference for the method of arbitrary rule. But the better is too often the enemy of the still better. Discussion, as the manifestation of intelligence in political life, stimulates publicity; by its means sore spots are brought to light that would otherwise remain hidden. It affords opportunity for promulgation of new ideas. Compared with despotic rule, it is an invitation to individuals to concern themselves with public affairs. But discussion and dialectic, however indispensable they are to the elaboration of ideas and policies after ideas are once put forth, are weak reeds to depend upon for systematic origination of comprehensive plans, the plans that are required if the problem of social organization is to be met. There was a time when discussion, the comparison of ideas already current so is to purify and clarify them, was thought to be sufficient in discovery of the structure and laws of physical nature. In the latter field, the method was displaced by that of experimental observation guided by comprehensive working hypotheses, and using all the resources made available by mathematics.

But we still depend upon the method of discussion, with only incidental scientific control, in politics. Our system of popular suffrage, immensely valuable as it is in comparison with what preceded it, exhibits the idea that intelligence is an individualistic possession, at best enlarged by public discussion. Existing political practice, with its complete ignoring of occupational groups and the organized knowledge and purposes that are involved in the existence of such groups, manifests a dependence upon a summation of individuals quantitatively, similar to Bentham's purely quantitative formula of the greatest sum of pleasures of the greatest possible number. The formation of parties or, as the eighteenth-century writers called them, factions, and the system of party government is the practically necessary counterweight to a numerical and atomistic individualism. The idea that the conflict of parties will, by means of public discussion, bring out necessary public truths is a kind of political watered-down version of the Hegelian dialectic, with its synthesis arrived at by a union of antithetical conceptions. The method has nothing in common with the procedure of organized cooperative inquiry which has won the triumphs of science in the field of physical nature. Intelligence in politics when it is identified with discussion means reliance upon symbols. The invention of language is probably the greatest single invention achieved by humanity. The development of political forms that promote the use of symbols in place of arbitrary power was another great invention. The nineteenth-century establishment of parliamentary institutions, written constitutions and the suffrage as means of political rule, is a tribute to the power of symbols. But symbols are significant only in connection with realities behind them. No intelligent observer can deny, I think, that they are often used in party politics as a substitute for realities instead of as means of contact with them. Popular literacy, in connection with the telegraph, cheap postage and the printing press, has enormously multiplied the number of those influenced. That which we term education has done a good deal to generate habits that put symbols in the place of realities. The forms of popular government make necessary the elaborate use of words to influence political action. "Propaganda" is the inevitable consequence of the combination of these influences and it extends to every area of life. Words not only take the place of realities but are themselves debauched. Decline in the prestige of suffrage and of parliamentary government are intimately associated with the belief, manifest in practice even if not expressed in words, that intelligence is an individual possession to be reached by means of verbal persuasion.

This fact suggests, by way of contrast, the genuine meaning of intelligence in connection with public opinion, sentiment and action. The crisis in democracy demands the substitution of the intelligence that is exemplified in scientific procedure for the kind of intelligence that is now accepted. The need for this change is not exhausted in the demand for greater honesty and impartiality, even though these qualities be now corrupted by discussion carried on mainly for purposes of party supremacy and for imposition of some special but concealed interest. These qualities need to be restored. But the need goes further. The social use of intelligence would remain deficient even if these moral traits were exalted, and yet intelligence continued to be identified simply with discussion and persuasion, necessary as are these things. Approximation to use of scientific method in investigation and of the engineering mind in the invention and projection of far-reaching social plans is demanded. The habit of considering social realities in terms of

cause and effect and social policies in terms of means and consequences is still inchoate. The contrast between the state of
intelligence in politics and in the physical control of nature is
to be taken literally. What has happened in this latter is the
outstanding demonstration of the meaning of organized intelligence. The combined effect of science and technology has
released more productive energies in a bare hundred years than
stands to the credit of prior human history in its entirety. Pro-
ductively it has multiplied nine million times in the last generation alone. The prophetic vision of Francis Bacon of subju-
gation of the energies of nature through change in methods of
inquiry has well-nigh been realized. The stationary engine, the
locomotive, the dynamo, the motor car, turbine, telegraph,
telephone, radio and moving picture are not the products of
either isolated individual minds nor of the particular economic
regime called capitalism. They are the fruit of methods that
first penetrated to the working causalities of nature and then
utilized the resulting knowledge in bold imaginative ventures
of invention and construction.

We hear a great deal in these days about class conflict. The
past history of man is held up to us as almost exclusively a record
of struggles between classes, ending in the victory of a class that
had been oppressed and the transfer of power to it. It is difficult
to avoid reading the past in terms of the contemporary scene.
Indeed, fundamentally it is impossible to avoid this course. With
a certain proviso, it is highly important that we are compelled to
follow this path. For the past as past is gone, save for esthetic
enjoyment and refreshment, while the present is with us. Knowledge of the past is significant only as it deepens and extends our
understanding of the present. Yet there is a proviso. We must
grasp the things that are most important in the present when we

turn to the past and not allow ourselves to be misled by secondary phenomena no matter how intense and immediately urgent they are. Viewed from this standpoint, the rise of scientific method and of technology based upon it is the genuinely active force in producing the vast complex of changes the world is now undergoing, not the class struggle whose spirit and method are opposed to science. If we lay hold upon the causal force exercised by this embodiment of intelligence we shall know where to turn for the means of directing further change.

When I say that scientific method and technology have been the active force in producing the revolutionary transformations society is undergoing, I do not imply no other forces have been at work to arrest, deflect and corrupt their operation. Rather this fact is positively implied. At this point, indeed, is located the conflict that underlies the confusions and uncertainties of the present scene. The conflict is between institutions and habits originating in the pre-scientific and pre-technological age and the new forces generated by science and technology. The application of science, to a considerable degree, even its own growth, has been conditioned by the system to which the name of capitalism is given, a rough designation of a complex of political and legal arrangements centering about a particular mode of economic relations. Because of the conditioning of science and technology by this setting, the second and humanly most important part of Bacon's prediction has so far largely missed realization. The conquest of natural energies has not accrued to the betterment of the common human estate in anything like the degree he anticipated.

Because of conditions that were set by the legal institutions and the moral ideas existing when the scientific and industrial revolutions came into being, the chief usufruct of the latter has been appropriated by a relatively small class. Industrial entre-preneurs have reaped out of all proportion to what they sowed. By obtaining private ownership of the means of production and exchange they deflected a considerable share of the results of increased productivity to their private pockets. This appro-priation was not the fruit of criminal conspiracy or of sinister intent. It was sanctioned not only by legal institutions of age-long standing but by the entire prevailing, moral code. The institution of private property long antedated feudal times. It is the institution with which men have lived, with few excep-tions, since the dawn of civilization. Its existence has deeply impressed itself upon mankind's moral conceptions. Moreover, the new industrial forces tended to break down many of the rigid class barriers that had been in force, and to give to millions a new outlook and inspire a new hope;—especially in this coun-try with no feudal background and no fixed class system.

Since the legal institutions and the patterns of mind char-acteristic of ages of civilization still endure, there exists the conflict that brings confusion into every phase of present life. The problem of bringing into being a new social orientation and organization is, when reduced to its ultimates, the problem of using the new resources of production, made possible by the advance of physical science, for social ends, for what Bentham called the greatest good of the greatest number. Institutional relationships fixed in the pre-scientific age stand in the way of accomplishing this great transformation. Lag in mental and moral patterns provides the bulwark of the older institutions; in expressing the past they still express present beliefs, outlooks and purposes. Here is the place where the problem of liberal-ism centers today.

The argument drawn from past history that radical change

must be effected by means of class struggle, culminating in open war, fails to discriminate between the two forces, one active, the other resistant and deflecting, that have produced the social scene in which we live. The active force is, as I have said, scientific method and technological application. The opposite force is that of older institutions and the habits that have grown up around them. Instead of discrimination between forces and distribution of their consequences, we find the two things lumped together. The compound is labeled the capitalistic or the bourgeois class, and to this class as a class is imputed all the important features of present industrialized society—much as the defenders of the régime of economic liberty exercised for private property are accustomed to attribute every improvement made in the last century and a half to the same capitalistic régime. Thus in orthodox communist literature, from the *Communist Manifesto* of 1848 to the present day, we are told that the bourgeoisie, the name for a distinctive class, has done this and that. It has, so it is said, given a cosmopolitan character to production and consumption; has destroyed the national basis of industry; has agglomerated population in urban centers; has transferred power from the country to the city, in the process of creating colossal productive force, its chief achievement. In addition, it has created crises of ever renewed intensity; has created imperialism of a new type in frantic effort to control raw materials and markets. Finally, it has created a new class, the proletariat, and has created it as a class having a common interest opposed to that of the bourgeoisie, and is giving an irresistible stimulus to its organization, first as a class and then as a political power. According to the economic version of the Hegelian dialectic, the bourgeois class is thus creating its own complete and polar opposite, and this in time will end the old power and rule. The class struggle of veiled civil war will finally burst into open revolution and the result will be either the common ruin of the contending parties or a revolutionary reconstitution of society at large through a transfer of power from one class to another.

The position thus sketched unites vast sweep with great simplicity. I am concerned with it here only as far as it emphasizes the idea of a struggle between classes, culminating in open and violent warfare as being the method for production of radical social change. For, be it noted, the issue is not whether some amount of violence will accompany the effectuation of radical change of institutions. The question is whether force or intelligence is to be the method upon which we consistently rely and to whose promotion we devote our energies. Insistence that the use of violent force is *inevitable* limits the use of available intelligence, for wherever the inevitable reigns intelligence cannot be used. Commitment to inevitability is always the fruit of dogma; intelligence does not pretend to *know* save as a result of experimentation, the opposite of preconceived dogma. Moreover, acceptance in advance of the inevitability of violence tends to produce the use of violence in cases where peaceful methods might otherwise avail. The curious fact is that while it is generally admitted that this and that particular social problem, say of the family, or railroads or banking, must be solved, if at all, by the method of intelligence, yet there is supposed to be some one all-inclusive social problem which can be solved only by the use of violence. This fact would be inexplicable were it not a conclusion from dogma as its premise.

It is frequently asserted that the method of experimental intelligence can be applied to physical facts because physical nature does not present conflicts of class interests, while it is inapplicable to society because the latter is so deeply marked by incompatible interests. It is then assumed that the "experimentalist" is one who has chosen to ignore the uncomfortable fact of conflicting interests. Of course, there *are* conflicting interests; otherwise there would be no social problems. The problem under discussion is precisely *how* conflicting claims are to be settled in the interest of the widest possible contribution to the interests of all—or at least of the great majority. The method of democracy—inasfar as it is that of organized intelligence—is to bring these conflicts out into the open where their special claims can be seen and appraised, where they can be discussed and judged in the light of more inclusive interests than are represented by either of them separately. There is, for example, a clash of interests between munition manufacturers and most of the rest of the population. The more the respective claims of the two are publicly and scientifically weighed, the more likely it is that the public interest will be disclosed and be made effective. There is an undoubted objective clash of interests between finance-capitalism that controls the means of production and whose profit is served by maintaining relative scarcity, and idle workers and hungry consumers. But what generates violent strife is failure to bring the conflict into the light of intelligence where the conflicting interests can be adjudicated in behalf of the interest of the great majority. Those most committed to the dogma of inevitable force recognize the need for intelligently discovering and expressing the dominant social interest up to a certain point and then draw back. The "experimentalist" is one who would see to it that the method depended upon by all in some degree in every democratic community be followed through to completion.

In spite of the existence of class conflicts, amounting at

times to veiled civil war, any one habituated to the use of the method of science will view with considerable suspicion the erection of actual human beings into fixed entities called classes, having no overlapping interests and so internally unified and externally separated that they are made the protagonists of history—itself hypothetical. Such an idea of classes is a survival of a rigid logic that once prevailed in the sciences of nature, but that no longer has any place there. This conversion of abstractions into entities smells more of a dialectic of concepts than of a realistic examination of facts, even though it makes more of an emotional appeal to many than do the results of the latter. To say that all past historic social progress has been the result of cooperation and not of conflict would be also an exaggeration. But exaggeration against exaggeration, it is the more reasonable of the two. And it is no exaggeration to say that the measure of civilization is the degree in which the method of cooperative intelligence replaces the method of brute conflict.

But the point I am especially concerned with just here is the indiscriminate lumping together as a single force of two different things—the results of scientific technology and of a legal system of property relations. It is science and technology that have had the revolutionary social effect while the legal system has been the relatively static element. According to the Marxians themselves, the economic foundations of society consist of two things, the forces of production on one side and, on the other side, the social relations of production, that is, the legal property system under which the former operates. The latter tags behind, and "revolutions" are produced by the power of the forces of production to change the system of institutional relations. But what are the modern forces of production save those of scientific technology? And what is scientific technology save a large-scale demonstration of organized intelligence in action?

It is quite true that what is happening socially is the result of the combination of the two factors, one dynamic, the other relatively static. If we choose to call the combination by the name of capitalism, then it is true, or a truism, that capitalism is the "cause" of all the important social changes that have occurred—an argument that the representatives of capitalism are eager to put forward whenever the increase of productivity is in question. But if we want to *understand*, and not just to paste labels, unfavorable or favorable as the case may be, we shall certainly begin and end with discrimination. Colossal increase in productivity, the bringing of men together in cities and large factories, the elimination of distance, the accumulation of capital, fixed and liquid—these things would have come about, at a certain stage, no matter what the established institutional system. They are the consequence of the new means of technological production. Certain other things have happened because of institutions and the habits of belief and character that accompany and support them. If we begin at this point, we shall see that the release of productivity is the product of cooperatively organized intelligence, and shall also see that the institutional framework is precisely that which is not subjected as yet, in any considerable measure, to the impact of inventive and constructive intelligence. That coercion and oppression on a large scale exist, no honest person can deny. But these things are not the product of science and technology but of the perpetuation of old institutions and patterns untouched by scientific method. The inference to be drawn is clear.

The argument, drawn from history, that great social changes have been effected only by violent means, needs considerable qualification, in view of the vast scope of changes that are taking place without the use of violence. But even if it be admitted to hold of the past, the conclusion that violence is the method now to be depended upon does not follow—unless one is committed to a dogmatic philosophy of history. The radical who insists that the future method of change must be like that of the past has much in common with the hide-bound reactionary who holds to the past as an ultimate fact. Both overlook the *fact that history in being a process of change generates change not only in details but also in the method of directing social change.* I recur to what I said at the beginning of this chapter. It is true that the social order is largely conditioned by the use of coercive force, bursting at times into open violence. But what is also true is that mankind now has in its possession a new method, that of cooperative and experimental science which expresses the method of intelligence. I should be meeting dogmatism with dogmatism if I asserted that the existence of this historically new factor completely invalidates all arguments drawn from the effect of force in the past. But it is within the bounds of reason to assert that the presence of this social factor demands that the present situation be analyzed on its own terms, and not be rigidly subsumed under fixed conceptions drawn from the past.

Any analysis made in terms of the present situation will not fail to note one fact that militates powerfully against arguments drawn from past use of violence. Modern warfare is destructive beyond anything known in older times. This increased destructiveness is due primarily, of course, to the fact that science has raised to a new pitch of destructive power all the agencies of armed hostility. But it also due to the much greater interdependence of all the elements of society. The bonds that hold modern communities and states together are as delicate as they are numerous. The self-sufficiency and independence of a local community, characteristic of more primitive societies, have disappeared in every highly industrialized country. The gulf that once separated the civilian population from the military has virtually gone. War involves paralysis of all normal social activities, and not merely the meeting of armed forces in the field. The *Communist Manifesto* presented two alternatives: *either* the revolutionary change and transfer of power to the proletariat, *or* the common ruin of the contending parties. Today, the civil war that would be adequate to effect transfer of power and a reconstitution of society at large, as understood by official Communists, would seem to present but one possible consequence: the ruin of all parties and the destruction of civilized life. This fact alone is enough to lead us to consider the potentialities of the method of intelligence.

The argument for putting chief dependence upon violence as the method of effecting radical change is, moreover, usually put in a way that proves altogether too much for its own case. It is said that the dominant economic class has all the agencies of power in its hands, directly the army, militia and police; indirectly, the courts, schools, press and radio. I shall not stop to analyze this statement. But if one admits it to be valid, the conclusion to be drawn is surely the folly of resorting to a use of force against force that is so well intrenched. The positive conclusion that emerges is that conditions that would promise success in the case of use of force are such as to make possible great change without any great recourse to such a method.[1]

---

1. It should be noted that Marx himself was not completely committed to the dogma of the inevitability of force as the means of effecting revolutionary changes in the system of "social relations." For at one time he contemplated that the change might occur in Great Britain and the United States, and possibly in Holland, by peaceful means.

Those who uphold the necessity of dependence upon violence usually much oversimplify the case by setting up a disjunction they regard as self-evident. They say that the sole alternative is putting our trust in parliamentary procedures as they now exist. This isolation of law-making from other social forces and agencies that are constantly operative is wholly unrealistic. Legislatures and congresses do not exist in a vacuum—not even the judges on the bench live in completely secluded sound-proof chambers. The assumption that it is possible for the constitution and activities of law-making bodies to persist unchanged while society itself is undergoing great change is an exercise in verbal formal logic.

It is true that in this country, because of the interpretations made by courts of a written constitution, our political institutions are unusually inflexible. It Is also true, as well as even more important (because it is a factor in causing this rigidity) that our institutions, democratic in form, tend to favor in substance a privileged plutocracy. Nevertheless, it is sheer defeatism to assume in advance of actual trial that democratic political institutions are incapable either of further development or of constructive social application. Even as they now exist, the forms of representative government are potentially capable of expressing the public will when that assumes anything like unification. And there is nothing inherent in them that forbids their supplementation by political agencies that represent definitely economic social interests, like those of producers and consumers.

The final argument in behalf of the use of intelligence is that as are the means used so are the actual ends achieved— that is, the consequences. I know of no greater fallacy than the claim of those who hold to the dogma of the necessity of brute force that this use will be the method of calling genuine democracy into existence—of which they profess themselves the simon-pure adherents. It requires an unusually credulous faith in the Hegelian dialectic of opposites to think that all of a sudden the use of force by a class will be transmuted into a democratic classless society. Force breeds counterforce; the Newtonian law of action and reaction still holds in physics, and violence is physical. To profess democracy as an ultimate ideal and the suppression of democracy as a means to the ideal may be possible in a country that has never known even rudimentary democracy, but when professed in a country that has anything of a genuine democratic spirit in its traditions, it signifies desire for possession and retention of power by a class, whether that class be called Fascist or Proletarian. In the light of what happens in non-democratic countries, it is pertinent to ask whether the rule of a class signifies the dictatorship of the majority, or dictatorship over the chosen class by a minority party; whether dissenters are allowed even within the class the party claims to represent; and whether the development of literature and the other arts proceeds according to a formula prescribed by a party in conformity with a doctrinaire dogma of history and of infallible leadership, or whether artists are free from regimentation? Until these questions are satisfactorily answered, it is permissible to look with considerable suspicion upon those who assert that suppression of democracy is the road to the adequate establishment of genuine democracy. The one exception—and that apparent rather than real—to dependence upon organized intelligence as the method for directing social change is found when society through an authorized majority has entered upon the path of social experimentation leading to great social change, and a minority refuses by force to permit the method of intelligent action to go into effect. Then force may be intelligently employed to subdue and disarm the recalcitrant minority.

There may be some who think I am unduly dignifying a position held by a comparatively small group by taking their arguments as seriously as I have done. But their position serves to bring into strong relief the alternatives before us. It makes clear the meaning of renascent liberalism. The alternatives are continuation of drift with attendant improvisations to meet special emergencies; dependence upon violence; dependence upon socially organized intelligence. The first two alternatives, however, are not mutually exclusive, for if things are allowed to drift the result may be some sort of social change effected by the use of force, whether so planned or not. Upon the whole, the recent policy of liberalism has been to further "social legislation"; that is, measures which add performance of social services to the older functions of government. The value of this addition is not to be despised. It marks a decided move away from *laissez faire* liberalism, and has considerable importance in educating the public mind to a realization of the possibilities of organized social control. It has helped to develop some of the techniques that in any case will be needed in a socialized economy. But the cause of liberalism will be lost for a considerable period if it is not prepared to go further and socialize the forces of production, now at hand, so that the liberty of individuals will be supported by the very structure of economic organization.

The ultimate place of economic organization in human life is to assure the secure basis for an ordered expression of individual capacity and for the satisfaction of the needs of man in noneconomic directions. The effort of mankind in connection with material production belongs, as I said earlier, among interests and activities that are, relatively speaking, routine in character, "routine" being defined as that which, without absorbing attention and energy, provides a constant basis for liberation of the values of intellectual, esthetic and companionship life. Every significant religious and moral teacher and prophet has asserted that the material is instrumental to the good life. Nominally at least, this idea is accepted by every civilized community. The transfer of the burden of material production from human muscles and brain to steam, electricity and chemical processes now makes possible the effective actualization of this ideal. Needs, wants and desires are always the moving force in generating creative action. When these wants are compelled by force of conditions to be directed for the most part, among the mass of mankind, into obtaining the means of subsistence, what should be a means becomes perforce an end in itself. Up to the present the new mechanical forces of production, which are the means of emancipation from this state of affairs, have been employed to intensify and exaggerate the reversal of the true relation between means and ends. Humanly speaking, I do not see how it would have been possible to avoid an epoch having this character. But its perpetuation is the cause of the continually growing social chaos and strife. Its termination cannot be effected by preaching to individuals that they should place spiritual ends above material means. It can be brought about by organized social reconstruction that puts the results of the mechanism of abundance at the free disposal of individuals. The actual corrosive "materialism" of our times does not proceed from science. It springs from the notion, sedulously cultivated by the class in power, that the creative capacities of individuals can be evoked and developed only in a struggle for material possessions and material gain. We either should surrender our professed belief in the supremacy of ideal and spiritual values and accommodate our beliefs to the predominant material orientation, or we should through organized endeavor institute the socialized economy of material security and plenty that will release human energy for pursuit of higher values.

Since liberation of the capacities of individuals for free, self-initiated expression is an essential part of the creed of liberalism, liberalism that is sincere must will the means that condition the achieving of its ends. Regimentation of material and mechanical forces is the only way by which the mass of individuals can be released from regimentation and consequent suppression of their cultural possibilities. The eclipse of liberalism is due to the fact that it has not faced the alternatives and adopted the means upon which realization of its professed aims depends. Liberalism can be true to its ideals only as it takes the course that leads to their attainment. The notion that organized social control of economic forces lies outside the historic path of liberalism shows that liberalism is still impeded by remnants of its earlier *laissez faire* phase, with its opposition of society and the individual. The thing which now dampens liberal ardor and paralyzes its efforts is the conception that liberty and development of individuality as ends exclude the use of organized social effort as means. Earlier liberalism regarded the separate and competing economic action of individuals as the means to social well-being as the end. We must reverse the perspective and see that socialized economy is the means of free individual development as the end.

That liberals are divided in outlook and endeavor while reactionaries are held together by community of interests and the ties of custom is well-nigh a commonplace. Organization of standpoint and belief among liberals can be achieved only in and by unity of endeavor. Organized unity of action attended by consensus of beliefs will come about in the degree in which social control of economic forces is made the goal of liberal action. The greatest educational power, the greatest force in shaping the dispositions and attitudes of individuals, is the social medium in which they live. The medium that now lies closest to us is that of unified action for the inclusive end of a socialized economy. The attainment of a state of society in which a basis of material security will release the powers of individuals for cultural expression is not the work of a day. But by concentrating upon the task of securing a socialized economy as the ground and medium for release of the impulses and capacities men agree to call ideal, the now scattered and often conflicting activities of liberals can be brought to effective unity.

It is no part of my task to outline in detail a program for renascent liberalism. But the question of "what is to be done" cannot be ignored. Ideas must be organized, and this organization implies an organization of individuals who hold these ideas and whose faith is ready to translate itself into action. Translation into action signifies that the general creed of liberalism be formulated as a concrete program of action. It is in organization for action that liberals are weak, and without this organization there is danger that democratic ideals may go by default. Democracy has been a fighting faith. When its ideals are reenforced by those of scientific method and experimental intelligence, it cannot be that it is incapable of evoking discipline, ardor and organization. To narrow the issue for the future to a struggle between Fascism and Communism is to invite a catastrophe that may carry civilization down in the struggle. Vital and courageous democratic liberalism is the one force that can surely avoid such a disastrous narrowing of the issue. I for one do not believe that Americans living in the tradition of Jefferson and Lincoln will weaken and give up without a whole-hearted effort to make democracy a living reality. This, I repeat, involves organization.

The question cannot be answered by argument. Experimental method means experiment, and the question can be answered only by trying, by organized effort. The reasons for making the trial are not abstract or recondite. They are found in the confusion, uncertainty and conflict that mark the modern world. The reasons for thinking that the effort if made will be successful are also not abstract and remote. They lie in what the method of experimental and cooperative intelligence has already accomplished in subduing to potential human use the energies of physical nature. In material production, the method of intelligence is now the established rule; to abandon it would be to revert to savagery. The task is to go on, and not backward, until the method of intelligence and experimental control is the rule in social relations and social direction. Either we take this road or we admit that the problem of social organization in behalf of human liberty and the flowering of human capacities is insoluble.

It would be fantastic folly to ignore or to belittle the obstacles that stand in the way. But what has taken place, also against great odds, in the scientific and industrial revolutions, is an accomplished fact; the way is marked out. It may be that the way will remain untrodden. If so, the future holds the menace of confusion moving into chaos, a chaos that will be externally masked for a time by an organization of force, coercive and violent, in which the liberties of men will all but disappear. Even so, the cause of the liberty of the human spirit, the cause of opportunity of human beings for full development of their powers, the cause for which liberalism enduringly stands, is too precious and too ingrained in the human constitution to be forever obscured. Intelligence after millions of years of errancy has found itself as a method, and it will not be lost forever in the blackness of night. The business of liberalism is to bend every energy and exhibit every courage so that these precious goods may not even be temporarily lost but be intensified and expanded here and now.

A COMMON FAITH

CONTENTS

1. RELIGION VERSES THE RELIGIOUS

NEVER before in history has mankind been so much of two minds, so divided into two camps, as it is today. Religions have traditionally been allied with ideas of the supernatural, and often have been based upon explicit beliefs about it. Today there are many who hold that nothing worthy of being called religious is possible apart from the supernatural. Those who hold this belief differ in many respects. They range from those who accept the dogmas and sacraments of the Greek and Roman Catholic church as the only sure means of access to the supernatural to the theist or mild deist. Between them are the many Protestant denominations who think the Scriptures, aided by a pure conscience, are adequate avenues to supernatural truth and power. But they agree in one point: the necessity for a Supernatural Being and for an immortality that is beyond the power of nature.

The opposed group consists of those who think the advance of culture and science has completely discredited the supernatural and with it all religions that were allied with belief in it. But they go beyond this point. The extremists in this group believe that with elimination of the supernatural not only must historic religions be dismissed but with them everything of a religious nature. When historical knowl-

edge has discredited the claims made for the supernatural character of the persons said to have founded
historic religions; when the supernatural inspiration
attributed to literatures held sacred has been riddled,
and when anthropological and psychological knowledge has disclosed the all-too-human source from
which religious beliefs and practices have sprung,
everything religious must, they say, also go.

There is one idea held in common by these two opposite groups: identification of the religious with the
supernatural. The question I shall raise in these
chapters concerns the ground for and the consequences of this identification: its reasons and its
value. In the discussion I shall develop another conception of the nature of the religious phase of experience, one that separates it from the supernatural
and the things that have grown up about it. I shall
try to show that these derivations are encumbrances
and that what is genuinely religious will undergo an
emancipation when it is relieved from them; that
then, for the first time, the religious aspect of experience will be free to develop freely on its own account.

This view is exposed to attack from both the other
camps. It goes contrary to traditional religions, including those that have the greatest hold upon the
religiously minded today. The view announced will
seem to them to cut the vital nerve of the religious
element itself in taking away the basis upon which
traditional religions and institutions have been
founded. From the other side, the position I am tak-

ing seems like a timid halfway position, a concession and compromise unworthy of thought that is thoroughgoing. It is regarded as a view entertained from mere tendermindedness, as an emotional hangover from childhood indoctrination, or even as a manifestation of a desire to avoid disapproval and curry favor.

The heart of my point, as far as I shall develop it in this first section, is that there is a difference between religion, *a* religion, and the religious; between anything that may be denoted by a noun substantive and the quality of experience that is designated by an adjective. It is not easy to find a definition of religion in the substantive sense that wins general acceptance. However, in the *Oxford Dictionary* I find the following: "Recognition on the part of man of some unseen higher power as having control of his destiny and as being entitled to obedience, reverence and worship."

This particular definition is less explicit in assertion of the supernatural character of the higher unseen power than are others that might be cited. It is, however, surcharged with implications having their source in ideas connected with the belief in the supernatural, characteristic of historic religions. Let us suppose that one familiar with the history of religions, including those called primitive, compares the definition with the variety of known facts and by means of the comparison sets out to determine just what the definition means. I think he will be struck by three facts that reduce the terms of the definition

to such a low common denominator that little meaning is left.

He will note that the "unseen powers" referred to
have been conceived in a multitude of incompatible
ways. Eliminating the differences, nothing is left
beyond the bare reference to something unseen and
powerful. This has been conceived as the vague and
undefined Mana of the Melanesians; the Kami of
primitive Shintoism; the fetish of the Africans;
spirits, having some human properties, that pervade
natural places and animate natural forces; the ultimate and impersonal principle of Buddhism; the un-
moved mover of Greek thought; the gods and semi-
divine heroes of the Greek and Roman Pantheons;
the personal and loving Providence of Christianity,
omnipotent, and limited by a corresponding evil
power; the arbitrary Will of Moslemism; the supreme legislator and judge of deism. And these are
but a few of the outstanding varieties of ways in
which the invisible power has been conceived.

There is no greater similarity in the ways in which
obedience and reverence have been expressed. There
has been worship of animals, of ghosts, of ancestors,
phallic worship, as well as of a Being of dread power
and of love and wisdom. Reverence has been expressed in the human sacrifices of the Peruvians and
Aztecs; the sexual orgies of some Oriental religions;
exorcisms and ablutions; the offering of the humble
and contrite mind of the Hebrew prophet, the elaborate rituals of the Greek and Roman Churches. Not
even sacrifice has been uniform; it is highly subli-

mated in Protestant denominations and in Moslemism. Where it has existed it has taken all kinds of
forms and been directed to a great variety of powers
and spirits. It has been used for expiation, for propitiation and for buying special favors. There is no
conceivable purpose for which rites have not been
employed.

Finally, there is no discernible unity in the moral
motivations appealed to and utilized. They have
been as far apart as fear of lasting torture, hope of
enduring bliss in which sexual enjoyment has sometimes been a conspicuous element; mortification of
the flesh and extreme asceticism; prostitution and
chastity; wars to extirpate the unbeliever; persecution to convert or punish the unbeliever, and philanthropic zeal; servile acceptance of imposed dogma,
along with brotherly love and aspiration for a reign
of justice among men.

I have, of course, mentioned only a sparse number
of the facts which fill volumes in any well-stocked
library. It may be asked by those who do not like to
look upon the darker side of the history of religions
why the darker facts should be brought up. We all
know that civilized man has a background of besti-
ality and superstition and that these elements are
still with us. Indeed, have not some religions, including the most influential forms of Christianity, taught
that the heart of man is totally corrupt? How could
the course of religion in its entire sweep not be
marked by practices that are shameful in their cruelty and lustfulness, and by beliefs that are degraded

and intellectually incredible? What else than what
we find could be expected, in the case of people having little knowledge and no secure method of knowing; with primitive institutions, and with so little
control of natural forces that they lived in a constant
state of fear?

I gladly admit that historic religions have been
relative to the conditions of social culture in which
peoples lived. Indeed, what I am concerned with is to
press home the logic of this method of disposal of
outgrown traits of past religions. Beliefs and practices in a religion that now prevails are by this logic
relative to the present state of culture. If so much
flexibility has obtained in the past regarding an unseen power, the way it affects human destiny, and the
attitudes we are to take toward it, why should it be
assumed that change in conception and action has
now come to an end? The logic involved in getting
rid of inconvenient aspects of past religions compels
us to inquire how much in religions now accepted are
survivals from outgrown cultures. It compels us to
ask what conception of unseen powers and our relations to them would be consonant with the best
achievements and aspirations of the present. It demands that in imagination we wipe the slate clean
and start afresh by asking what would be the idea of
the unseen, of the manner of its control over us and
the ways in which reverence and obedience would be
manifested, if whatever is basically religious in experience had the opportunity to express itself free
from all historic encumbrances.

So we return to the elements of the definition that has been given. What boots it to accept, in defense of the universality of religion, a definition that applies equally to the most savage and degraded beliefs and practices that have related to unseen powers and to noble ideals of a religion having the greatest share of moral content? There are two points involved. One of them is that there is nothing left worth preserving in the notions of unseen powers, controlling human destiny to which obedience, reverence and worship are due, if we glide silently over the nature that has been attributed to the powers, the radically diverse ways in which they have been supposed to control human destiny, and in which submission and awe have been manifested. The other point is that when we begin to select, to choose, and say that some present ways of thinking about the unseen powers are better than others; that the reverence shown by a free and self-respecting human being is better than the servile obedience rendered to an arbitrary power by frightened men; that we should believe that control of human destiny is exercised by a wise and loving spirit rather than by madcap ghosts or sheer force—when I say, we begin to choose, we have entered upon a road that has not yet come to an end. We have reached a point that invites us to proceed farther.

For we are forced to acknowledge that concretely there is no such thing as religion in the singular. There is only a multitude of religions. "Religion" is a strictly collective term and the collection it stands for is not even of the kind illustrated in textbooks of logic. It has not the unity of a regiment or assembly but that of any miscellaneous aggregate. Attempts to prove the universality prove too much or too little. It is probable that religions have been universal in the sense that all the peoples we know anything about have had *a* religion. But the differences among them are so great and so shocking that any common element that can be extracted is meaningless. The idea that religion is universal proves too little in that the older apologists for Christianity seem to have been better advised than some modern ones in condemning every religion but one as an impostor, as at bottom some kind of demon worship or at any rate a superstitious figment. Choice among religions is imperative, and the necessity for choice leaves nothing of any force in the argument from universality. Moreover, when once we enter upon the road of choice, there is at once presented a possibility not yet generally realized.

For the historic increase of the ethical and ideal content of religions suggests that the process of purification may be carried further. It indicates that further choice is imminent in which certain values and functions in experience may be selected. This possibility is what I had in mind in speaking of the difference between the religious and a religion. I am not proposing a religion, but rather the emancipation of elements and outlooks that may be called religious. For the moment we have a religion, whether that of the Sioux Indian or of Judaism or of Christianity, that moment the ideal factors in experience that may be called religious take on a load that is not inherent in them, a load of current beliefs and of institutional practices that are irrelevant to them.

I can illustrate what I mean by a common phenomenon in contemporary life. It is widely supposed that a person who does not accept any religion is thereby shown to be a non-religious person. Yet it is conceivable that the present depression in religion is closely connected with the fact that religions now prevent, because of their weight of historic encumbrances, the religious quality of experience from coming to consciousness and finding the expression that is appropriate to present conditions, intellectual and moral. I believe that such is the case. I believe that many persons are so repelled from what exists as a religion by its intellectual and moral implications, that they are not even aware of attitudes in themselves that if they came to fruition would be genuinely religious. I hope that this remark may help make clear what I mean by the distinction between "religion" as a noun substantive and "religious" as adjectival.

To be somewhat more explicit, a religion (and as I have just said there is no such thing as religion in general) always signifies a special body of beliefs and practices having some kind of institutional organization, loose or tight. In contrast, the adjective "religious" denotes nothing in the way of a specifiable entity, either institutional or as a system of beliefs. It does not denote anything to which one can

specifically point as one can point to this and that
historic religion or existing church. For it does not
denote anything that can exist by itself or that can
be organized into a particular and distinctive form
of existence. It denotes attitudes that may be taken
toward every object and every proposed end or ideal.

Before, however, I develop my suggestion that realization of the distinction just made would operate
to emancipate the religious quality from encumbrances that now smother or limit it, I must refer to
a position that in some respects is similar in words
to the position I have taken, but that in fact is a
whole world removed from it. I have several times
used the phrase "religious elements of experience."
Now at present there is much talk, especially in liberal circles, of religious experience as vouching for
the authenticity of certain beliefs and the desirability
of certain practices, such as particular forms of
prayer and worship. It is even asserted that religious
experience is the ultimate basis of religion itself. The
gulf between this position and that which I have
taken is what I am now concerned to point out.

Those who hold to the notion that there is a definite kind of experience which is itself religious, by
that very fact make out of it something specific, as
a kind of experience that is marked off from experience as æsthetic, scientific, moral, political; from experience as companionship and friendship. But "religious" as a quality of experience signifies something that may belong to all these experiences. It is
the polar opposite of some type of experience that

can exist by itself. The distinction comes out clearly
when it is noted that the concept of this distinct kind
of experience is used to validate a belief in some
special kind of object and also to justify some special
kind of practice.

For there are many religionists who are now dis-
satisfied with the older "proofs" of the existence of
God, those that go by the name of ontological, cosmological and teleological. The cause of the dissatisfaction is perhaps not so much the arguments that
Kant used to show the insufficiency of these alleged
proofs, as it is the growing feeling that they are too
formal to offer any support to religion in action.
Anyway, the dissatisfaction exists. Moreover, these
religionists are moved by the rise of the experimental
method in other fields. What is more natural and
proper, accordingly, than that they should affirm
they are just as good empiricists as anybody else—
indeed, as good as the scientists themselves? As the
latter rely upon certain kinds of experience to prove
the existence of certain kinds of objects, so the religionists rely upon a certain kind of experience to
prove the existence of the object of religion, especially the supreme object, God.

The discussion may be made more definite by introducing, at this point, a particular illustration of
this type of reasoning. A writer says: "I broke down
from overwork and soon came to the verge of nervous
prostration. One morning after a long and sleepless
night . . . I resolved to stop drawing upon myself
so continuously and begin drawing upon God. I de-

termined to set apart a quiet time every day in which
I could relate my life to its ultimate source, regain
the consciousness that in God I live, move and have
my being. That was thirty years ago. Since then I
have had literally not one hour of darkness or despair."

This is an impressive record. I do not doubt its
authenticity nor that of the experience related. It illustrates a religious aspect of experience. But it illustrates also the use of that quality to carry a super-
imposed load of a particular religion. For having
been brought up in the Christian religion, its subject interprets it in the terms of the personal God
characteristic of that religion. Taoists, Buddhists,
Moslems, persons of no religion including those who
reject all supernatural influence and power, have had
experiences similar in their effect. Yet another author
commenting upon the passage says: "The religious
expert can be more sure that this God exists than he
can of either the cosmological God of speculative sur-
mise or the Christlike God involved in the validity of
moral optimism," and goes on to add that such experiences "mean that God the savior, the power that
gives victory over sin on certain conditions that man
can fulfill, is an existent, accessible and scientifically
knowable reality." It should be clear that this inference is sound only if the conditions, of whatever sort,
that produce the effect are called "God." But most
readers will take the inference to mean that the existence of a particular Being, of the type called "God"

in the Christian religion, is proved by a method akin to that of experimental science.

In reality, the only thing that can be said to be "proved" is the existence of some complex of conditions that have operated to effect an adjustment in life, an orientation, that brings with it a sense of security and peace. The particular interpretation given to this complex of conditions is not inherent in the experience itself. It is derived from the culture with which a particular person has been imbued. A fatalist will give one name to it; a Christian Scientist another, and the one who rejects all supernatural being still another. The determining factor in the interpretation of the experience is the particular doctrinal apparatus into which a person has been inducted. The emotional deposit connected with prior teaching floods the whole situation. It may readily confer upon the experience such a peculiarly sacred preciousness that all inquiry into its causation is barred. The stable outcome is so invaluable that the cause to which it is referred is usually nothing but a reduplication of the thing that has occurred, plus some name that has acquired a deeply emotional quality.

The intent of this discussion is not to deny the genuineness of the result nor its importance in life. It is not, save incidentally, to point out the possibility of a purely naturalistic explanation of the event. My purpose is to indicate what happens when religious experience is already set aside as something *sui generis*. The actual religious quality in the experience described is the *effect* produced, the better adjustment in life and its conditions, not the manner and cause of its production. The way in which the experience operated, its function, determines its religious value. If the reorientation actually occurs, it, and the sense of security and stability accompanying it, are forces on their own account. It takes place in different persons in a multitude of ways. It is sometimes brought about by devotion to a cause; sometimes by a passage of poetry that opens a new perspective; sometimes as was the case with Spinoza— deemed an atheist in his day—through philosophical reflection.

The difference between an experience having a religious force because of what it does in and to the processes of living and religious experience as a separate kind of thing gives me occasion to refer to a previous remark. If this function were rescued through emancipation from dependence upon specific types of beliefs and practices, from those elements that constitute a religion, many individuals would find that experiences having the force of bringing about a better, deeper and enduring adjustment in life are not so rare and infrequent as they are commonly supposed to be. They occur frequently in connection with many significant moments of living. The idea of invisible powers would take on the meaning of all the conditions of nature and human association that support and deepen the sense of values which carry one through periods of darkness and despair to such an extent that they lose their usual depressive character.

I do not suppose for many minds the dislocation of the religious from a religion is easy to effect. Tradition and custom, especially when emotionally charged, are a part of the habits that have become one with our very being. But the possibility of the transfer is demonstrated by its actuality. Let us then for the moment drop the term "religious," and ask what are the attitudes that lend deep and enduring support to the processes of living. I have, for example, used the words "adjustment" and "orientation." What do they signify?.

While the words "accommodation," "adaptation," and "adjustment" are frequently employed as synonyms, attitudes exist that are so different that for the sake of clear thought they should be discriminated. There are conditions we meet that cannot be changed. If they are particular and limited, we modify our own particular attitudes in accordance with them. Thus we accommodate ourselves to changes in weather, to alterations in income when we have no other recourse. When the external conditions are lasting we become inured, habituated, or, as the process is now often called, conditioned. The two main traits of this attitude, which I should like to call accommodation, are that it affects *particular* modes of conduct, not the entire self, and that the process is mainly *passive*. It may, however, become general and then it becomes fatalistic resignation or submission. There are other attitudes toward the environment that are also particular but that are more active. We re-act against conditions and endeavor to change them to meet our wants and demands. Plays in a foreign language are "adapted" to meet the needs of an American audience. A house is rebuilt to suit changed conditions of the household; the telephone is invented to serve the demand for speedy communication at a distance; dry soils are irrigated so that they may bear abundant crops. Instead of accommodating ourselves to conditions, we modify conditions so that they will be accommodated to our wants and purposes. This process may be called adaptation.

Now both of these processes are often called by the more general name of adjustment. But there are also changes in ourselves in relation to the world in which we live that are much more inclusive and deep seated. They relate not to this and that want in relation to this and that condition of our surroundings, but pertain to our being in its entirety. Because of their scope, this modification of ourselves is enduring. It lasts through any amount of vicissitude of circumstances, internal and external. There is a composing and harmonizing of the various elements of our being such that, in spite of changes in the special conditions that surround us, these conditions are also arranged, settled, in relation to us. This attitude includes a note of submission. But it is voluntary, not externally imposed; and as voluntary it is something more than a mere Stoical resolution to endure unperturbed throughout the buffetings of fortune. It is more outgoing, more ready and glad, than the latter attitude, and it is more active than the former. And in calling it voluntary, it is not meant that it depends upon a particular resolve or volition. It is a change *of* will conceived as the organic plenitude of our being, rather than any special change *in* will.

It is the claim of religions that they effect this generic and enduring change in attitude. I should like to turn the statement around and say that whenever this change takes place there is a definitely religious attitude. It is not *a* religion that brings it about, but when it occurs, from whatever cause and by whatever means, there is a religious outlook and function. As I have said before, the doctrinal or intellectual apparatus and the institutional accretions that grow up are, in a strict sense, adventitious to the intrinsic quality of such experiences. For they are affairs of the traditions of the culture with which individuals are inoculated. Mr. Santayana has connected the religious quality of experience with the imaginative, as that is expressed in poetry. "Religion and poetry," he says, "are identical in essence, and differ merely in the way in which they are attached to practical affairs. Poetry is called religion when it intervenes in life, and religion, when it merely supervenes upon life, is seen to be nothing but poetry." The difference between intervening *in* and supervening *upon* is as important as is the identity set forth. Imagination may play upon life or it may enter profoundly into it. As Mr. Santayana puts it, "poetry has a universal and a moral function," for "its highest power lies in its relevance to the ideals and purposes of life." Except as it intervenes, "all observation is observation of brute fact, all discipline is mere repression, until these facts digested and this discipline embodied in humane impulses become the starting point for a creative movement of the imagination, the firm basis for ideal constructions in society, religion, and art."

If I may make a comment upon this penetrating insight of Mr. Santayana, I would say that the difference between imagination that only supervenes and imagination that intervenes is the difference between one that completely interpenetrates all the elements of our being and one that is interwoven with only special and partial factors. There actually occurs extremely little observation of brute facts merely for the sake of the facts, just as there is little discipline that is repression and nothing but repression. Facts are usually observed with reference to some practical end and purpose, and that end is presented only imaginatively. The most repressive discipline has some end in view to which there is at least imputed an ideal quality; otherwise it is purely sadistic. But in such cases of observation and discipline imagination is limited and partial. It does not extend far; it does not permeate deeply and widely.

The connection between imagination and the harmonizing of the self is closer than is usually thought. The idea of a whole, whether of the whole personal being or of the world, is an imaginative, not a literal, idea. The limited world of our observation and reflection becomes the Universe only through imaginative extension. It cannot be apprehended in knowledge nor realized in reflection. Neither observation, thought, nor practical activity can attain that complete unification of the self which is called a whole. The *whole* self is an ideal, an imaginative projection. Hence the idea of a thoroughgoing and deep-seated harmonizing of the self with the Universe (as a name for the totality of conditions with which the self is connected) operates only through imagination —which is one reason why this composing of the self is not voluntary in the sense of an act of special volition or resolution. An "adjustment" possesses the will rather than is its express product. Religionists have been right in thinking of it as an influx from sources beyond conscious deliberation and purpose— a fact that helps explain, psychologically, why it has so generally been attributed to a supernatural source and that, perhaps, throws some light upon the reference of it by William James to unconscious factors. And it is pertinent to note that the unification of the self throughout the ceaseless flux of what it does, suffers, and achieves, cannot be attained in terms of itself. The self is always directed toward something beyond itself and so its own unification depends upon the idea of the integration of the shifting scenes of the world into that imaginative totality we call the Universe.

The intimate connection of imagination with ideal elements in experience is generally recognized. Such is not the case with respect to its connection with faith. The latter has been regarded as a substitute for knowledge, for sight. It is defined, in the Christian religion, as *evidence* of things not seen. The implication is that faith is a kind of anticipatory vision of things that are now invisible because of the limitations of our finite and erring nature. Because it is a substitute for knowledge, its material and object are intellectual in quality. As John Locke summed up the matter, faith is "assent to a proposition . . . on the credit of its proposer." Religious faith is then given to a body of propositions as true on the credit of their supernatural author, reason coming in to demonstrate the reasonableness of giving such credit. Of necessity there results the development of theologies, or bodies of systematic propositions, to make explicit in organized form the content of the propositions to which belief is attached and assent given. Given the point of view, those who hold that religion necessarily implies a theology are correct.

But belief or faith has also a moral and practical import. Even devils, according to the older theologians, believe—and tremble. A distinction was made, therefore, between "speculative" or intellectual belief and an act called "justifying" faith. Apart from any theological context, there is a difference between belief that is a conviction that some end should be supreme over conduct, and belief that some object or being exists as a truth for the intellect. Conviction in the moral sense signifies being conquered, vanquished, in our active nature by an ideal end; it signifies acknowledgment of its rightful claim over our desires and purposes. Such acknowledgment is practical, not primarily intellectual. It goes beyond evidence that can be presented to *any* possible observer. Reflection, often long and arduous, may be involved in arriving at the conviction, but the import of thought is not exhausted in discovery of evidence that can justify intellectual assent. The authority of an ideal over choice and conduct is the authority of an ideal, not of a fact, of a truth guaranteed to intellect, not of the status of the one who propounds the truth.

Such moral faith is not easy. It was questioned of old whether the Son of Man should find faith on the earth in his coming. Moral faith has been bolstered by all sorts of arguments intended to prove that its object is not ideal and that its claim upon us is not primarily moral or practical, since the ideal in question is already embedded in the existent frame of things. It is argued that the ideal is already the final reality at the heart of things that exist, and that only our senses or the corruption of our natures prevent us from apprehending its prior existential being. Starting, say, from such an idea as that justice is more than a moral ideal because it is embedded in the very make-up of the actually existent world, men have gone on to build up vast intellectual schemes, philosophies, and theologies, to prove that ideals are real not as ideals but as antecedently existing actualities. They have failed to see that in converting moral realities into matters of intellectual assent they have evinced lack of *moral* faith. Faith that something should be in existence as far as lies in our power is changed into the intellectual belief that it is already in existence. When physical existence does not bear out the assertion, the physical is subtly changed into the metaphysical. In this way, moral faith has been inextricably tied up with intellectual beliefs about the supernatural.

The tendency to convert ends of moral faith and action into articles of an intellectual creed has been furthered by a tendency of which psychologists are well aware. What we ardently desire to have thus and so, we tend to believe is already so. Desire has a powerful influence upon intellectual beliefs. Moreover, when conditions are adverse to realization of the objects of our desire—and in the case of significant ideals they are extremely adverse—it is an easy way out to assume that after all they are already embodied in the ultimate structure of what is, and that appearances to the contrary are *merely* appearances. Imagination then merely supervenes and is freed from the responsibility for intervening. Weak natures take to reverie as a refuge as strong ones do to fanaticism. Those who dissent are mourned over by the first class and converted through the use of force by the second.

What has been said does not imply that all moral faith in ideal ends is by virtue of that fact religious in quality. The religious is "morality touched by emotion" only when the ends of moral conviction arouse emotions that are not only intense but are actuated and supported by ends so inclusive that they unify the self. The inclusiveness of the end in relation to both self and the "universe" to which an inclusive self is related is indispensable. According to the best authorities, "religion" comes from a root that means being bound or tied. Originally, it meant being bound by vows to a particular way of life—as *les religieux* were monks and nuns who had assumed certain vows. The religious attitude signifies something that is bound through imagination to a *general* attitude. This comprehensive attitude, moreover, is much broader than anything indicated by "moral" in its usual sense. The quality of attitude is displayed in art, science and good citizenship.

If we apply the conception set forth to the terms of the definition earlier quoted, these terms take on a new significance. An unseen power controlling our destiny becomes the power of an ideal. All possibilities, as possibilities, are ideal in character. The artist, scientist, citizen, parent, as far as they are actuated by the spirit of their callings, are controlled by the unseen. For all endeavor for the better is moved by faith in what is possible, not by adherence to the actual. Nor does this faith depend for its moving power upon intellectual assurance or belief that the things worked for must surely prevail and come into embodied existence. For the authority of the object to determine our attitude and conduct, the right that is given it to claim our allegiance and devotion is based on the intrinsic nature of the ideal. The outcome, given our best endeavor, is not with us. The inherent vice of all intellectual schemes of idealism is that they convert the idealism of action into a system of beliefs

about antecedent reality. The character assigned this
reality is so different from that which observation
and reflection lead to and support that these schemes
inevitably glide into alliance with the supernatural.

All religions, marked by elevated ideal quality,
have dwelt upon the power of religion to introduce
perspective into the piecemeal and shifting episodes
of existence. Here too we need to reverse the ordinary
statement and say that whatever introduces genuine
perspective is religious, not that religion is something
that introduces it. There can be no doubt (referring
to the second element of the definition) of our dependence upon forces beyond our control. Primitive
man was so impotent in the face of these forces that,
especially in an unfavorable natural environment,
fear became a dominant attitude, and, as the old say-
ing goes, fear created the gods.

With increase of mechanisms of control, the element of fear has, relatively speaking, subsided. Some
optimistic souls have even concluded that the forces
about us are on the whole essentially benign. But
every crisis, whether of the individual or of the community, reminds man of the precarious and partial
nature of the control he exercises. When man, individually and collectively, has done his uttermost, conditions that at different times and places have given
rise to the ideas of Fate and Fortune, of Chance and
Providence, remain. It is the part of manliness to insist upon the capacity of mankind to strive to direct
natural and social forces to humane ends. But unqualified absolutistic statements about the omnipo-

tence of such endeavors reflect egoism rather than intelligent courage.

The fact that human destiny is so interwoven with forces beyond human control renders it unnecessary to suppose that dependence and the humility that accompanies it have to find the particular channel that is prescribed by traditional doctrines. What is especially significant is rather the form which the sense of dependence takes. Fear never gave stable perspective in the life of anyone. It is dispersive and withdrawing. Most religions have in fact added rites of communion to those of expiation and propitiation. For our dependence is manifested in those relations to the environment that support our undertakings and aspirations as much as it is in the defeats inflicted upon us. The essentially unreligious attitude is that which attributes human achievement and purpose to man in isolation from the world of physical nature and his fellows. Our successes are dependent upon the coöperation of nature. The sense of the dignity of human nature is as religious as is the sense of awe and reverence when it rests upon a sense of human nature as a coöperating part of a larger whole. Natural piety is not of necessity either a fatalistic acquiescence in natural happenings or a romantic idealization of the world. It may rest upon a just sense of nature as the whole of which we are parts, while it also recognizes that we are parts that are marked by intelligence and purpose, having the capacity to strive by their aid to bring conditions into greater consonance with what is humanly desirable. Such piety is an inherent constituent of a just perspective in life.

Understanding and knowledge also enter into a perspective that is religious in quality. Faith in the continued disclosing of truth through directed co-operative human endeavor is more religious in quality than is any faith in a completed revelation. It is of course now usual to hold that revelation is not completed in the sense of being ended. But religions hold that the essential framework is settled in its significant moral features at least, and that new elements that are offered must be judged by conformity to this framework. Some fixed doctrinal apparatus is necessary for *a* religion. But faith in the possibilities of continued and rigorous inquiry does not limit access to truth to any channel or scheme of things. It does not first say that truth is universal and then add there is but one road to it. It does not depend for assurance upon subjection to any dogma or item of doctrine. It trusts that the natural interactions between man and his environment will breed more intelligence and generate more knowledge provided the scientific methods that define intelligence in operation are pushed further into the mysteries of the world, being themselves promoted and improved in the operation. There is such a thing as faith in intelligence becoming religious in quality—a fact that perhaps explains the efforts of some religionists to disparage the possibilities of intelligence as a force. They properly feel such faith to be a dangerous rival.

Lives that are consciously inspired by loyalty to such ideals as have been mentioned are still comparatively infrequent to the extent of that comprehensiveness and intensity which arouse an ardor religious in function. But before we infer the incompetency of such ideals and of the actions they inspire, we should at least ask ourselves how much of the existing situation is due to the fact that the religious factors of experience have been drafted into supernatural channels and thereby loaded with irrelevant encumbrances. A body of beliefs and practices that are apart from the common and natural relations of mankind must, in the degree in which it is influential, weaken and sap the force of the possibilities inherent in such relations. Here lies one aspect of the emancipation of the religious from religion.

Any activity pursued in behalf of an ideal end against obstacles and in spite of threats of personal loss because of conviction of its general and enduring value is religious in quality. Many a person, inquirer, artist, philanthropist, citizen, men and women in the humblest walks of life, have achieved, without presumption and without display, such unification of themselves and of their relations to the conditions of existence. It remains to extend their spirit and inspiration to ever wider numbers. If I have said anything about religions and religion that seems harsh, I have said those things because of a firm belief that the claim on the part of religions to possess a monopoly of ideals and of the supernatural means by which alone, it is alleged, they can be furthered, stands in the way of the realization of distinctively religious values inherent in natural experience. For that reason, if for no other, I should be sorry if any were misled by the frequency with which I have employed the adjective "religious" to conceive of what I have said as a disguised apology for what have passed as religions. The opposition between religious values as I conceive them and religions is not to be bridged. Just because the release of these values is so important, their identification with the creeds and cults of religions must be dissolved.

2. FAITH AND IT'S OBJECT

ALL religions, as I pointed out in the preceding chapter, involve specific intellectual beliefs, and they attach—some greater, some less—importance to assent to these doctrines as true, true in the intellectual sense. They have literatures held especially sacred, containing historical material with which the validity of the religions is connected. They have developed a doctrinal apparatus it is incumbent upon "believers" (with varying degrees of strictness in different religions) to accept. They also insist that there is some special and isolated channel of access to the truths they hold.

No one will deny, I suppose, that the present crisis in religion is intimately bound up with these claims. The skepticism and agnosticism that are rife and that from the standpoint of the religionist are fatal to the religious spirit are directly bound up with the intellectual contents, historical, cosmological, ethical, and theological, asserted to be indispensable in everything religious. There is no need for me here to go with any minuteness into the causes that have generated doubt and disbelief, uncertainty and rejection, as to these contents. It is enough to point out that all the beliefs and ideas in question, whether having to do with historical and literary matters, or with astronomy, geology and biology, or with the creation and structure of the world and man, are connected with the supernatural, and that this connection is the factor that has brought doubt upon them; the factor that from the standpoint of historic and institutional religions is sapping the religious life itself.

The obvious and simple facts of the case are that some views about the origin and constitution of the world and man, some views about the course of human history and personages and incidents in that history, have become so interwoven with religion as to be identified with it. On the other hand, the growth of knowledge and of its methods and tests has been such as to make acceptance of these beliefs increasingly onerous and even impossible for large numbers of cultivated men and women. With such persons, the result is that the more these ideas are used as the basis and justification of a religion, the more dubious that religion becomes.

Protestant denominations have largely abandoned the idea that particular ecclesiastic sources can authoritatively determine cosmic, historic and theological beliefs. The more liberal among them have at least mitigated the older belief that individual hardness and corruption of heart are the causes of intellectual rejection of the intellectual apparatus of the Christian religion. But these denominations have also, with exceptions numerically insignificant, retained a certain indispensable minimum of intellectual content. They ascribe peculiar religious force to certain literary documents and certain historic personages. Even when they have greatly reduced the bulk of intellectual content to be accepted, they have insisted at least upon theism and the immortality of the individual.

It is no part of my intention to rehearse in any detail the weighty facts that collectively go by the name of the conflict of science and religion—a conflict that is not done away with by calling it a conflict of science with theology, as long as even a minimum of intellectual assent is prescribed as essential. The impact of astronomy not merely upon the older cosmogony of religion but upon elements of creeds dealing with historic events—witness the idea of ascent into heaven—is familiar. Geological discoveries have displaced creation myths which once bulked large. Biology has revolutionized conceptions of soul and mind which once occupied a central place in religious beliefs and ideas, and this science has made a profound impression upon ideas of sin, redemption, and immortality. Anthropology, history and literary criticism have furnished a radically different version of the historic events and personages upon which Christian religions have built. Psychology is already opening to us natural explanations of phenomena so extraordinary that once their supernatural origin was, so to say, the natural explanation.

The significant bearing for my purpose of all this is that new methods of inquiry and reflection have become for the educated man today the final arbiter of all questions of fact, existence, and intellectual assent. Nothing less than a revolution in the "seat of intellectual authority" has taken place. This revolution, rather than any particular aspect of its impact upon this and that religious belief, is the central thing. In this revolution, every defeat is a stimulus to renewed inquiry; every victory won is the open door to more discoveries, and every discovery is a new seed planted in the soil of intelligence, from which grow fresh plants with new fruits. The mind of man is being habituated to a new method and ideal: There is but one sure road of access to truth—the road of patient, coöperative inquiry operating by means of observation, experiment, record and controlled reflection.

The scope of the change is well illustrated by the fact that whenever a particular outpost is surrendered it is usually met by the remark from a liberal theologian that the particular doctrine or supposed historic or literary tenet surrendered was never, after all, an intrinsic part of religious belief, and that without it the true nature of religion stands out more clearly than before. Equally significant is the growing gulf between fundamentalists and liberals in the churches. What is not realized—although perhaps it is more definitely seen by fundamentalists than by liberals—is that the issue does not concern this and that piecemeal *item* of belief, but centers in the question of the method by which any and every item of intellectual belief is to be arrived at and justified.

The positive lesson is that religious qualities and values if they are real at all are not bound up with any single item of intellectual assent, not even that of the existence of the God of theism; and that, under existing conditions, the religious function in experience can be emancipated only through surrender of the whole notion of special truths that are religious by their own nature, together with the idea of peculiar avenues of access to such truths. For were we to admit that there is but one method for ascertaining fact and truth—that conveyed by the word "scientific" in its most general and generous sense—no discovery in any branch of knowledge and inquiry could then disturb the faith that is religious. I should describe this faith as the unification of the self through allegiance to inclusive ideal ends, which imagination presents to us and to which the human will responds as worthy of controlling our desires and choices.

It is probably impossible to imagine the amount of intellectual energy that has been diverted from normal processes of arriving at intellectual conclusions because it has gone into rationalization of the doctrines entertained by historic religions. The set that has thus been given the general mind is much more harmful, to my mind, than are the consequences of any one particular item of belief, serious as have been those flowing from acceptance of some of them. The modern liberal version of the intellectual content of Christianity seems to the modern mind to be more rational than some of the earlier doctrines that have been reacted against. Such is not the case in fact. The theological philosophers of the Middle Ages had no greater difficulty in giving rational form to all the doctrines of the Roman church than has the liberal theologian of today in formulating and justifying intellectually the doctrines he entertains. This statement is as applicable to the doctrine of continuing miracles, penance, indulgences, saints and angels, etc., as to the trinity, incarnation, atonement, and the sacraments. The fundamental question, I repeat, is not of this and that article of intellectual belief but of intellectual habit, method and criterion.

One method of swerving aside the impact of changed knowledge and method upon the intellectual content of religion is the method of division of territory and jurisdiction into two parts. Formerly these were called the realm of nature and the realm of grace. They are now often known as those of revelation and natural knowledge. Modern religious liberalism has no definite names for them, save, perhaps, the division, referred to in the last chapter, between scientific and religious experience. The implication is that in one territory the supremacy of scientific knowledge must be acknowledged, while there is another region, not very precisely defined, of intimate personal experience wherein other methods and criteria hold sway.

This method of justifying the peculiar and legitimate claim of certain elements of belief is always open to the objection that a positive conclusion is drawn from a negative fact. Existing ignorance or backwardness is employed to assert the existence of a division in the nature of the subject-matter dealt with. Yet the gap may only reflect, at most, a limitation now existing but in the future to be done away with. The argument that because some province or aspect of experience has not yet been "invaded" by scientific methods, it is not subject to them, is as old as it is dangerous. Time and time again, in some particular reserved field, it has been invalidated. Psychology is still in its infancy. He is bold to the point of rashness who asserts that intimate personal experience will never come within the ken of natural knowledge.

It is more to the present point, however, to consider the region that is claimed by religionists as a special reserve. It is mystical experience. The difference, however, between mystic experience and the theory about it that is offered to us must be noted. The experience is a fact to be inquired into. The theory, like any theory, is an interpretation of the fact. The idea that by its very nature the experience is a veridical realization of the direct presence of God does not rest so much upon examination of the facts as it does upon importing into their interpretation a conception that is formed outside them. In its dependence upon a prior conception of the supernatural, which is the thing to be proved, it begs the question.

History exhibits many types of mystic experience, and each of these types is contemporaneously explained by the concepts that prevail in the culture and the circle in which the phenomena occur. There are mystic crises that arise, as among some North American Indian tribes, induced by fasting. They are accompanied by trances and semi-hysteria. Their purpose is to gain some special power, such perhaps as locating a person who is lost or finding objects that have been secreted. There is the mysticism of Hindoo practice now enjoying some vogue in Western countries. There is the mystic ecstasy of Neoplatonism with its complete abrogation of the self and absorption into an impersonal whole of Being. There is the mysticism of intense æsthetic experience independent of any theological or metaphysical interpretation. There is the heretical mysticism of William Blake. There is the mysticism of sudden unreasoning fear in which the very foundations seem shaken beneath one—to mention but a few of the types that may be found.

What common element is there between, say, the Neoplatonic conception of a super-divine Being wholly apart from human needs and conditions and the medieval theory of an immediate union that is fostered through attention to the sacraments or through concentration upon the heart of Jesus? The contemporary emphasis of some Protestant theologians upon the sense of inner personal communion with God, found in religious experience, is almost as far away from medieval Christianity as it is from Neoplatonism or Yoga. Interpretations of the experience have not grown from the experience itself with the aid of such scientific resources as may be available. They have been imported by borrowing without criticism from ideas that are current in the surrounding culture.

The mystic states of the shaman and of some

North American Indians are frankly techniques for gaining a special power—*the* power as it is conceived by some revivalist sects. There is no especial intellectual objectification accompanying the experience. The knowledge that is said to be gained is not that of Being but of particular secrets and occult modes of operation. The aim is not to gain knowledge of superior divine power, but to get advice, cures for the sick, prestige, etc. The conception that mystic experience is a normal mode of religious experience by which we may acquire knowledge of God and divine things is a nineteenth-century interpretation that has gained vogue in direct ratio to the decline of older methods of religious apologetics.

There is no reason for denying the existence of experiences that are called mystical. On the contrary, there is every reason to suppose that, in some degree of intensity, they occur so frequently that they may be regarded as normal manifestations that take place at certain rhythmic points in the movement of experience. The assumption that denial of a particular interpretation of their objective content proves that those who make the denial do not have the experience in question, so that if they had it they would be equally persuaded of its objective source in the presence of God, has no foundation in fact. As with every empirical phenomenon, the occurrence of the state called mystical is simply an occasion for inquiry into its mode of causation. There is no more reason for converting the experience itself into an immediate knowledge of its cause than in the case of

an experience of lightning or any other natural occurrence.

My purpose, then, in this brief reference to mysticism is not to throw doubt upon the existence of
particular experiences called mystical. Nor is it to
propound any theory to account for them. I have referred to the matter merely as an illustration of the
general tendency to mark off two distinct realms in
one of which science has jurisdiction, while in the
other, special modes of immediate knowledge of religious objects have authority. This dualism as it
operates in contemporary interpretation of mystic
experience in order to validate certain beliefs is but a
reinstatement of the old dualism between the natural
and the supernatural, in terms better adapted to the
cultural conditions of the present time. Since it is the
conception of the supernatural that science calls in
question, the circular nature of this type of reasoning is obvious.

Apologists for a religion often point to the shift
that goes on in scientific ideas and materials as evidence of the unreliability of science as a mode of
knowledge. They often seem peculiarly elated by the
great, almost revolutionary, change in fundamental
physical conceptions that has taken place in science
during the present generation. Even if the alleged
unreliability were as great as they assume (or even
greater), the question would remain: Have we any
other recourse for knowledge? But in fact they miss
the point. Science is not constituted by any particular body of subject-matter. It is constituted by a

method, a method of changing beliefs by means of
tested inquiry as well as of arriving at them. It is its
glory, not its condemnation, that its subject-matter
develops as the method is improved. There is no special subject-matter of belief that is sacrosanct. The
identification of science with a particular set of beliefs and ideas is itself a hold-over of ancient and
still current dogmatic habits of thought which are
opposed to science in its actuality and which science
is undermining.

For scientific method is adverse not only to dogma
but to doctrine as well, provided we take "doctrine"
in its usual meaning—a body of definite beliefs that
need only to be taught and learned as true. This
negative attitude of science to doctrine does not indicate indifference to truth. It signifies supreme loyalty to the method by which truth is attained. The
scientific-religious conflict ultimately is a conflict between allegiance to this method and allegiance to
even an irreducible minimum of belief so fixed in advance that it can never be modified.

The method of intelligence is open and public. The
doctrinal method is limited and private. This limitation persists even when knowledge of the truth that
is religious is said to be arrived at by a special mode
of experience, that termed "religious." For the latter is assumed to be a very special kind of experience.
To be sure it is asserted to be open to all who obey
certain conditions. Yet the mystic experience yields,
as we have seen, various results in the way of belief
to different persons, depending upon the surround-

ing culture of those who undergo it. As a method, it lacks the public character belonging to the method of intelligence. Moreover, when the experience in question does not yield consciousness of the presence of God, in the sense that is alleged to exist, the retort is always at hand that it is not a genuine religious experience. For by definition, only that experience *is* religious which arrives at this particular result. The argument is circular. The traditional position is that some hardness or corruption of heart prevents one from having the experience. Liberal religionists are now more humane. But their logic does not differ.

It is sometimes held that beliefs about religious matters are symbolic, like rites and ceremonies. This view may be an advance upon that which holds to their literal objective validity. But as usually put forward it suffers from an ambiguity. Of what are the beliefs symbols? Are they symbols of things experienced in other modes than those set apart as religious, so that the things symbolized have an independent standing? Or are they symbols in the sense of standing for some transcendental reality—transcendental because not being the subject-matter of experience generally? Even the fundamentalist admits a certain quality and degree of symbolism in the latter sense in objects of religious belief. For he holds that the objects of these beliefs are so far beyond finite human capacity that our beliefs must be couched in more or less metaphorical terms. The conception that faith is the best available substitute for knowledge in our present estate still attaches to

the notion of the symbolic character of the materials
of faith; unless by ascribing to them a symbolic nature we mean that these materials stand for something that is verifiable in general and public experience.

Were we to adopt the latter point of view, it would
be evident not only that the intellectual articles of a
creed must be understood to be symbolic of moral
and other ideal values, but that the facts taken to be
historic and used as concrete evidence of the intellectual articles are themselves symbolic. These articles of a creed present events and persons that have
been made over by the idealizing imagination in the
interest, at their best, of moral ideals. Historic personages in their divine attributes are materializations
of the ends that enlist devotion and inspire endeavor.
They are symbolic of the reality of ends moving us
in many forms of experience. The ideal values that
are thus symbolized also mark human experience in
science and art and the various modes of human association: they mark almost everything in life that
rises from the level of manipulation of conditions as
they exist. It is admitted that the objects of religion
are ideal in contrast with our present state. What
would be lost if it were also admitted that they have
authoritative claim upon conduct just because they
are ideal? The assumption that these objects of religion exist already in some realm of Being seems to
add nothing to their force, while it weakens their
claim over us as ideals, in so far as it bases that claim
upon matters that are intellectually dubious. The

question narrows itself to this: Are the ideals that
move us genuinely ideal or are they ideal only in
contrast with our present estate?

The import of the question extends far. It determines the meaning given to the word "God." On one
score, the word can mean only a particular Being.
On the other score, it denotes the unity of all ideal
ends arousing us to desire and actions. Does the unification have a claim upon our attitude and conduct
because it is already, apart from us, in realized existence, or because of its own inherent meaning and
value? Suppose for the moment that the word "God"
means the ideal ends that at a given time and place
one acknowledges as having authority over his volition and emotion, the values to which one is su-
premely devoted, as far as these ends, through imagination, take on unity. If we make this supposition,
the issue will stand out clearly in contrast with the
doctrine of religions that "God" designates some
kind of Being having prior and therefore non-ideal
existence.

The word "non-ideal" is to be taken literally in regard to some religions that have historically existed,
to all of them as far as they are neglectful of moral
qualities in their divine beings. It does not apply in
the same *literal* way to Judaism and Christianity.
For they have asserted that the Supreme Being has
moral and spiritual attributes. But it applies to them
none the less in that these moral and spiritual characters are thought of as properties of a particular
existence and are thought to be of religious value for

us because of this embodiment in such an existence. Here, as far as I can see, is the ultimate issue as to the difference between *a* religion and the religious as a function of experience.

The idea that "God" represents a unification of ideal values that is essentially imaginative in origin when the imagination supervenes in conduct is attended with verbal difficulties owing to our frequent use of the word "imagination" to denote fantasy and doubtful reality. But the reality of ideal ends as ideals is vouched for by their undeniable power in action. An ideal is not an illusion because imagination is the organ through which it is apprehended. For *all* possibilities reach us through the imagination. In a definite sense the only meaning that can be assigned the term "imagination" is that things unrealized in fact come home to us and have power to stir us. The unification effected through imagination is not fanciful, for it is the reflex of the unification of practical and emotional attitudes. The unity signifies not a single Being, but the unity of loyalty and effort evoked by the fact that many ends are one in the power of their ideal, or imaginative, quality to stir and hold us.

We may well ask whether the power and significance in life of the traditional conceptions of God are not due to the ideal qualities referred to by them, the hypostatization of them into an existence being due to a conflux of tendencies in human nature that converts the object of desire into an antecedent reality (as was mentioned in the previous chapter) with beliefs that have prevailed in the cultures of the past. For in the older cultures the idea of the supernatural was "natural," in the sense in which "natural" signifies something customary and familiar. It seems more credible that religious persons have been supported and consoled by the reality with which ideal values appeal to them than that they have been upborne by sheer matter of fact existence. That, when once men are inured to the idea of the union of the ideal and the physical, the two should be so bound together in emotion that it is difficult to institute a separation, agrees with all we know of human psychology.

The benefits that will accrue, however, from making the separation are evident. The dislocation frees the religious values of experience once for all from matters that are continually becoming more dubious. With that release there comes emancipation from the necessity of resort to apologetics. The reality of ideal ends and values in their authority over us is an undoubted fact. The validity of justice, affection, and that intellectual correspondence of our ideas with realities that we call truth, is so assured in its hold upon humanity that it is unnecessary for the religious attitude to encumber itself with the apparatus of dogma and doctrine. Any other conception of the religious attitude, when it is adequately analyzed, means that those who hold it care more for force than for ideal values—since all that an Existence can add is force to establish, to punish, and to reward. There are, indeed, some persons who frankly say that their own faith does not require any guarantee that moral values are backed up by physical force, but who hold that the masses are so backward that ideal values will not affect their conduct unless in the popular belief these values have the sanction of a power that can enforce them and can execute justice upon those who fail to comply.

There are some persons, deserving of more respect, who say: "We agree that the beginning must be made with the primacy of the ideal. But why stop at this point? Why not search with the utmost eagerness and vigor for all the evidence we can find, such as is supplied by history, by presence of design in nature, which may lead on to the belief that the ideal is already extant in a Personality having objective existence?"

One answer to the question is that we are involved by this search in all the problems of the existence of evil that have haunted theology in the past and that the most ingenious apologetics have not faced, much less met. If these apologists had not identified the existence of ideal goods with that of a Person supposed to originate and support them—a Being, moreover, to whom omnipotent power is attributed— the problem of the occurrence of evil would be gratuitous. The significance of ideal ends and meanings is, indeed, closely connected with the fact that there are in life all sorts of things that are evil to us because we would have them otherwise. Were existing conditions wholly good, the notion of possibilities to be realized would never emerge.

But the more basic answer is that while if the search is conducted upon a strictly empirical basis there is no reason why it should not take place, as a matter of fact it is always undertaken in the interest of the supernatural. Thus it diverts attention and energy from ideal values and from the exploration of actual conditions by means of which they may be promoted. History is testimony to this fact. Men have never fully used the powers they possess to advance the good in life, because they have waited upon some power external to themselves and to nature to do the work they are responsible for doing. Dependence upon an external power is the counterpart of surrender of human endeavor. Nor is emphasis on exercising our own powers for good an egoistical or a sentimentally optimistic recourse. It is not the first, for it does not isolate man, either individually or collectively, from nature. It is not the second, because it makes no assumption beyond that of the need and responsibility for human endeavor, and beyond the conviction that, if human desire and endeavor were enlisted in behalf of natural ends, conditions would be bettered. It involves no expectation of a millennium of good.

Belief in the supernatural as a necessary power for apprehension of the ideal and for practical attachment to it has for its counterpart a pessimistic belief in the corruption and impotency of natural means. That is axiomatic in Christian dogma. But this apparent pessimism has a way of suddenly changing into an exaggerated optimism. For according to the terms of the doctrine, if the faith in the supernatural is of the required order, regeneration at once takes place. Goodness, in all essentials, is thereby established; if not, there is proof that the established relation to the supernatural has been vitiated. This romantic optimism is one cause for the excessive attention to individual salvation characteristic of traditional Christianity. Belief in a sudden and complete transmutation through conversion and in the objective efficacy of prayer, is too easy a way out of difficulties. It leaves matters in general just about as they were before; that is, sufficiently bad so that there is additional support for the idea that only supernatural aid can better them. The position of natural intelligence is that there exists a *mixture* of good and evil, and that reconstruction in the direction of the good which is indicated by ideal ends, must take place, if at all, through continued co-operative effort. There is at least enough impulse toward justice, kindliness, and order so that if it were mobilized for action, not expecting abrupt and complete transformation to occur, the disorder, cruelty, and oppression that exist would be reduced.

The discussion has arrived at a point where a more fundamental objection to the position I am taking needs consideration. The misunderstanding upon which this objection rests should be pointed out. The view I have advanced is sometimes treated as if the identification of the divine with ideal ends left the ideal wholly without roots in existence and without support from existence. The objection implies that

my view commits one to such a separation of the ideal
and the existent that the ideal has no chance to find
lodgment even as a seed that might grow and bear
fruit. On the contrary, what I have been criticizing
is the *identification* of the ideal with a particular
Being, especially when that identification makes necessary the conclusion that this Being is outside of
nature, and what I have tried to show is that the
ideal itself has its roots in natural conditions; it
emerges when the imagination idealizes existence by
laying hold of the possibilities offered to thought and
action. There are values, goods, actually realized
upon a natural basis—the goods of human association, of art and knowledge. The idealizing imagination seizes upon the most precious things found in the
climacteric moments of experience and projects
them. We need no external criterion and guarantee
for their goodness. They are had, they exist as good,
and out of them we frame our ideal ends.

Moreover, the ends that result from our projection
of experienced goods into objects of thought, desire
and effort exist, only they exist *as* ends. Ends, purposes, exercise determining power in human conduct.
The aims of philanthropists, of Florence Nightin-
gale, of Howard, of Wilberforce, of Peabody, have
not been idle dreams. They have modified institutions. Aims, ideals, do not exist simply in "mind";
they exist in character, in personality and action.
One might call the roll of artists, intellectual inquirers, parents, friends, citizens who are neighbors,
to show that purposes exist in an *operative* way.

What I have been objecting to, I repeat, is not the idea that ideals are linked with existence and that they themselves exist, through human embodiment, as forces, but the idea that their authority and value depend upon some prior complete embodiment—as if the efforts of human beings in behalf of justice, or knowledge or beauty, depended for their effectiveness and validity upon assurance that there already existed in some supernal region a place where criminals are humanely treated, where there is no serfdom or slavery, where all facts and truths are already discovered and possessed, and all beauty is eternally displayed in actualized form.

The aims and ideals that move us are generated through imagination. But they are not made out of imaginary stuff. They are made out of the hard stuff of the world of physical and social experience. The locomotive did not exist before Stevenson, nor the telegraph before the time of Morse. But the conditions for their existence were there in physical material and energies and in human capacity. Imagination seized hold upon the idea of a rearrangement of existing things that would evolve new objects. The same thing is true of a painter, a musician, a poet, a philanthropist, a moral prophet. The new vision does not arise out of nothing, but emerges through seeing, in terms of possibilities, that is, of imagination, old things in new relations serving a new end which the new end aids in creating.

Moreover the process of creation is experimental and continuous. The artist, scientific man, or good citizen, depends upon what others have done before him and are doing around him. The sense of new values that become ends to be realized arises first in dim and uncertain form. As the values are dwelt upon and carried forward in action they grow in definiteness and coherence. Interaction between aim and existent conditions improves and tests the ideal; and conditions are at the same time modified. Ideals change as they are applied in existent conditions. The process endures and advances with the life of humanity. What one person and one group accomplish becomes the standing ground and starting point of those who succeed them. When the vital factors in this natural process are generally acknowledged in emotion, thought and action, the process will be both accelerated and purified through elimination of that irrelevant element that culminates in the idea of the supernatural. When the vital factors attain the religious force that has been drafted into supernatural religions, the resulting reinforcement will be incalculable.

These considerations may be applied to the idea of God, or, to avoid misleading conceptions, to the idea of the divine. This idea is, as I have said, one of ideal possibilities unified through imaginative realization and projection. But this idea of God, or of the divine, is also connected with all the natural forces and conditions—including man and human association—that promote the growth of the ideal and that further its realization. We are in the presence neither of ideals completely embodied in existence nor yet of ideals that are mere rootless ideals, fantasies, utopias. For there are forces in nature and society that generate and support the ideals. They are further unified by the action that gives them coherence and solidity. It is this *active* relation between ideal and actual to which I would give the name "God." I would not insist that the name *must* be given. There are those who hold that the associations of the term with the supernatural are so numerous and close that any use of the word "God" is sure to give rise to misconception and be taken as a concession to traditional ideas.

They may be correct in this view. But the facts to which I have referred are there, and they need to be brought out with all possible clearness and force. There exist concretely and experimentally goods— the values of art in all its forms, of knowledge, of effort and of rest after striving, of education and fellowship, of friendship and love, of growth in mind and body. These goods are there and yet they are relatively embryonic. Many persons are shut out from generous participation in them; there are forces at work that threaten and sap existent goods as well as prevent their expansion. A clear and intense conception of a union of ideal ends with actual conditions is capable of arousing steady emotion. It may be fed by every experience, no matter what its material.

In a distracted age, the need for such an idea is urgent. It can unify interests and energies now dispersed; it can direct action and generate the heat of emotion and the light of intelligence. Whether one gives the name "God" to this union, operative in thought and action, is a matter for individual decision. But the *function* of such a working union of the ideal and actual seems to me to be identical with the force that has in fact been attached to the conception of God in all the religions that have a spiritual content; and a clear idea of that function seems to me urgently needed at the present time.

The sense of this union may, with some persons, be furthered by mystical experiences, using the term "mystical" in its broadest sense. That result depends largely upon temperament. But there is a marked difference between the union associated with mysticism and the union which I had in mind. There is nothing mystical about the latter; it is natural and moral. Nor is there anything mystical about the perception or consciousness of such union. Imagination of ideal ends pertinent to actual conditions represents the fruition of a disciplined mind. There is, indeed, even danger that resort to mystical experiences will be an escape, and that its result will be the passive feeling that the union of actual and ideal is already accomplished. But in fact this union is active and practical; it is a *uniting*, not something given.

One reason why personally I think it fitting to use the word "God" to denote that uniting of the ideal and actual which has been spoken of, lies in the fact that aggressive atheism seems to me to have something in common with traditional supernaturalism. I do not mean merely that the former is mainly so negative that it fails to give positive direction to thought, though that fact is pertinent. What I have in mind especially is the exclusive preoccupation of both militant atheism and supernaturalism with man in isolation. For in spite of supernaturalism's reference to something beyond nature, it conceives of this earth as the moral center of the universe and of man as the apex of the whole scheme of things. It regards the drama of sin and redemption enacted within the isolated and lonely soul of man as the one thing of ultimate importance. Apart from man, nature is held either accursed or negligible. Militant atheism is also affected by lack of natural piety. The ties binding man to nature that poets have always celebrated are passed over lightly. The attitude taken is often that of man living in an indifferent and hostile world and issuing blasts of defiance. A religious attitude, however, needs the sense of a connection of man, in the way of both dependence and support, with the enveloping world that the imagination feels is a universe. Use of the words "God" or "divine" to convey the union of actual with ideal may protect man from a sense of isolation and from consequent despair or defiance.

In any case, whatever the name, the meaning is selective. For it involves no miscellaneous worship of everything in general. It selects those factors in existence that generate and support our idea of good as an end to be striven for. It excludes a multitude of forces that at any given time are irrelevant to this function. Nature produces whatever gives reinforce-

ment and direction but also what occasions discord
and confusion. The "divine" is thus a term of human
choice and aspiration. A humanistic religion, if it
excludes our relation to nature, is pale and thin, as
it is presumptuous, when it takes humanity as an object of worship. Matthew Arnold's conception of a
"power not ourselves" is too narrow in its reference
to operative and sustaining conditions. While it is
selective, it is too narrow in its basis of selection—
righteousness. The conception thus needs to be widened in two ways. The powers that generate and support the good as experienced and as ideal, work
within as well as without. There seems to be a remi-
niscence of an external Jehovah in Arnold's statement. And the powers work to enforce other values
and ideals than righteousness. Arnold's sense of an
opposition between Hellenism and Hebraism resulted
in exclusion of beauty, truth, and friendship from
the list of the consequences toward which powers
work within and without.

In the relation between nature and human ends
and endeavors, recent science has broken down the
older dualism. It has been engaged in this task for
three centuries. But as long as the conceptions of
science were strictly mechanical (mechanical in the
sense of assuming separate things acting upon one
another purely externally by push and pull), religious apologists had a standing ground in pointing
out the differences between man and physical nature.
The differences could be used for arguing that something supernatural had intervened in the case of

man. The recent acclaim, however, by apologists for religion of the surrender by science of the classic type of mechanicalism* seems ill-advised from their own point of view. For the change in the modern scientific view of nature simply brings man and nature nearer together. We are no longer compelled to choose between explaining away what is distinctive in man through reducing him to another form of a mechanical model and the doctrine that something literally supernatural marks him off from nature. The less mechanical—in its older sense—physical nature is found to be, the closer is man to nature.

In his fascinating book, *The Dawn of Conscience*, James Henry Breasted refers to Haeckel as saying that the question he would most wish to have answered is this: Is the universe friendly to man? The question is an ambiguous one. Friendly to man in what respect? With respect to ease and comfort, to material success, to egoistic ambitions? Or to his aspiration to inquire and discover, to invent and create, to build a more secure order for human existence? In whatever form the question be put, the answer cannot in all honesty be an unqualified and absolute one. Mr. Breasted's answer, as a historian, is that nature has been friendly to the emergence and development of conscience and character. Those who will have all or nothing cannot be satisfied with this answer. Emergence and growth are not enough for

---

* I use this term because science has not abandoned its beliefs in working mechanisms in giving up the idea that they are of the nature of a strictly mechanical contact of discrete things.

them. They want something more than growth accompanied by toil and pain. They want final achievement. Others who are less absolutist may be content to think that, morally speaking, growth is a higher value and ideal than is sheer attainment. They will remember also that growth has not been confined to conscience and character; that it extends also to discovery, learning and knowledge, to creation in the arts, to furtherance of ties that hold men together in mutual aid and affection. These persons at least will be satisfied with an intellectual view of the religious function that is based on continuing choice directed toward ideal ends.

For, I would remind readers in conclusion, it is the intellectual side of the religious attitude that I have been considering. I have suggested that the religious element in life has been hampered by conceptions of the supernatural that were imbedded in those cultures wherein man had little control over outer nature and little in the way of sure method of inquiry and test. The crisis today as to the intellectual content of religious belief has been caused by the change in the intellectual climate due to the increase of our knowledge and our means of understanding. I have tried to show that this change is not fatal to the religious values in our common experience, however adverse its impact may be upon historic religions. Rather, provided that the methods and results of intelligence at work are frankly adopted, the change is liberating.

It clarifies our ideals, rendering them less subject

to illusion and fantasy. It relieves us of the incubus of thinking of them as fixed, as without power of growth. It discloses that they develop in coherence and pertinency with increase of natural intelligence. The change gives aspiration for natural knowledge a definitely religious character, since growth in understanding of nature is seen to be organically related to the formation of ideal ends. The same change enables man to select those elements in natural conditions that may be organized to support and extend the sway of ideals. All purpose is selective, and all intelligent action includes deliberate choice. In the degree in which we cease to depend upon belief in the supernatural, selection is enlightened and choice can be made in behalf of ideals whose inherent relations to conditions and consequences are understood. Were the naturalistic foundations and bearings of religion grasped, the religious element in life would emerge from the throes of the crisis in religion. Religion would then be found to have its natural place in every aspect of human experience that is concerned with estimate of possibilities, with emotional stir by possibilities as yet unrealized, and with all action in behalf of their realization. All that is significant in human experience falls within this frame.

3. THE HUMAN ABODE OF THE
RELIGIOUS FUNCTION

IN discussing the intellectual content of religion
before considering religion in its social connections, I did not follow the usual temporal order.
Upon the whole, collective modes of practice either
come first or are of greater importance. The core of
religions has generally been found in rites and ceremonies. Legends and myths grow up in part as deco-
rative dressings, in response to the irrepressible
human tendency toward story-telling, and in part
as attempts to explain ritual practices. Then as culture advances, stories are consolidated, and theogo-
nies and cosmogonies are formed—as with the Baby-
lonians, Egyptians, Hebrews and Greeks. In the case
of the Greeks, the stories of creation and accounts
of the constitution of the world were mainly poetic
and literary, and philosophies ultimately developed
from them. In most cases, legends along with rites
and ceremonies came under the guardianship of a
special body, the priesthood, and were subject to the
special arts which it possessed. A special group was
set aside as the responsible owners, protectors, and
promulgators of the corpus of beliefs.

But the formation of a special social group having a peculiar relation to both the practices and the

beliefs of religion is but part of the story. In the widest perspective, it is the less important part. The more significant point as regards the social import of religion is that the priesthoods were official representatives of some community, tribe, city-state or empire. Whether there was a priesthood or not, individuals who were members of a community were born into a religious community as they were into social and political organization. Each social group had its own divine beings who were its founders and protectors. Its rites of sacrifice, purification, and communion were manifestations of organized civic life. The temple was a public institution, the focus of the worship of the community; the influence of its practices extended to all the customs of the community, domestic, economic, and political. Even wars between groups were usually conflicts of their respective deities.

An individual did not join a church. He was born and reared in a community whose social unity, organization and traditions were symbolized and celebrated in the rites, cults and beliefs of a collective religion. Education was the induction of the young into community activities that were interwoven at every point with customs, legends and ceremonies intimately connected with and sanctioned by a religion. There are a few persons, especially those brought up in Jewish communities in Russia, who can understand without the use of imagination what a religion means socially when it permeates all the customs and activities of group life. To most of us

in the United States such a situation is only a remote
historic episode.

The change that has taken place in conditions once
universal and now infrequent is in my opinion the
greatest change that has occurred in religion in all
history. The intellectual conflict of scientific and
theological beliefs has attracted much more attention. It is still near the focus of attention. But the
change in the social center of gravity of religion has
gone on so steadily and is now so generally accomplished that it has faded from the thought of most
persons, save perhaps the historians, and even they
are especially aware of it only in its political aspect.
For the conflict between state and church still continues in some countries.

There are even now persons who are born into a
particular church, that of their parents, and who
take membership in it almost as a matter of course;
indeed, the fact of such membership may be an important, even a determining, factor in an individual's
whole career. But the thing new in history, the thing
once unheard of, is that the organization in question
is a *special* institution within a secular community.
Even where there are established churches, they are
constituted by the state and may be unmade by the
state. Not only the national state but other forms of
organization among groups have grown in power
and influence at the expense of organizations built
upon and about a religion. The correlate of this
fact is that membership in associations of the latter
type is more and more a matter of the voluntary

choice of individuals, who may tend to accept re-
sponsibilities imposed by the church but who accept
them of their own volition. If they do accept them,
the organization they join is, in many nations, char-
tered under a general corporation law of the political and secular entity.

The shift in what I have called the social center of
gravity accompanies the enormous expansion of associations formed for educational, political, economic, philanthropic and scientific purposes, which
has occurred independently of any religion. These
social modes have grown so much that they exercise
the greater hold upon the thought and interest of
most persons, even of those holding membership in
churches. This positive extension of interests which,
from the standpoint of a religion, are non-religious,
is so great that in comparison with it the direct effect
of science upon the creeds of religion seems to me of
secondary importance.

I say, the *direct* effect; for the indirect effect of
science in stimulating the growth of competing organizations is enormous. Changes that are purely intellectual affect at most but a small number of specialists. They are secondary to consequences brought
about through impact upon the *conditions* under
which human beings associate with one another. Invention and technology, in alliance with industry and
commerce, have, needless to say, profoundly affected
these underlying conditions of association. Every
political and social problem of the present day reflects this indirect influence, from unemployment to

banking, from municipal administration to the great migration of peoples made possible by new modes of transportation, from birth control to foreign commerce and war. The social changes that have come about through application of the new knowledge affect everyone, whether he is aware or not of the source of the forces that play upon him. The effect is the deeper, indeed, because so largely unconscious. For, to repeat what I have said, the *conditions* under which people meet and act together have been modified.

The fundamentalist in religion is one whose beliefs in intellectual content have hardly been touched by scientific developments. His notions about heaven and earth and man, as far as their bearing on religion is concerned, are hardly more affected by the work of Copernicus, Newton, and Darwin than they are by that of Einstein. But his actual life, in what he does day by day and in the contacts that are set up, has been radically changed by political and economic changes that have followed from applications of science. As far as strictly intellectual changes are concerned, creeds display great power of accommodation; their articles undergo insensible change of perspective; emphases are altered, and new meanings creep in. The Catholic Church, particularly, has shown leniency in dealing with intellectual deviations as long as they do not touch discipline, rites, and sacraments.

Among the laity only a small number, the more highly educated section, is directly affected by

changes in scientific beliefs. Certain ideas recede
more or less into the background but are not seriously challenged; nominally they are accepted.
Probably most educated people thought the conception of biological evolution had been accepted as a
commonplace until legislation in Tennessee and the
Scopes trial brought about an acute crisis that revealed how far that was from being the case. Within
an ecclesiastic organization, on the other hand, the
class of professionals does not sense the change in
perspective and emphasis of values in the general
mind until some acute situation reveals it. Then they
vigorously deny the validity of the new interests that
have arisen. But since they are working against interests rather than merely against ideas, their desperate efforts are not convincing except for those
already convinced.

Changes in practice that affect collective life go
deep and extend far. They have been operating ever
since the time we call the Middle Ages. The Renaissance was essentially a new birth of secularism. The
development of the idea of "natural religion," characteristic of the eighteenth century, was a protest
against control by ecclesiastic bodies—a movement
foreshadowed in this respect by the growth of "independent" religious societies in the preceding century.
But natural religion no more denied the intellectual
validity of supernatural ideas than did the growth
of independent congregations. It attempted rather to
justify theism and immortality on the basis of the
natural reason of the individual. The transcendental-

ism of the nineteentn century was a further move in
the same general direction, a movement in which
"reason" took on a more romantic, more colorful, and
more collective form. It asserted the diffusion of the
supernatural through secular life.

These movements and others not mentioned are the
intellectual reflex of the greatest revolution that has
taken place in religions during the thousands of
years that man has been upon earth. For, as I have
said, this change has to do with the *social* place and
function of religion. Even the hold of the supernatural upon the general mind has become more and
more disassociated from the power of ecclesiastic organization—that is, of any particular form of communal organization. Thus the very idea that was
central in religions has more and more oozed away,
so to speak, from the guardianship and care of any
particular social institution. Even more important
is the fact that a steady encroachment upon ecclesiastic institutions of forms of association once regarded as secular has altered the way in which men
spend their time in work, recreation, citizenship, and
political action. The essential point is not just that
secular organizations and actions are legally or externally severed from the control of the church, but
that interests and values unrelated to the offices of
any church now so largely sway the desires and aims
of even believers.

The individual believer may indeed carry the disposition and motivation he has acquired through
affiliation with a religious organization into his po-

litical action, into his connection with schools, even into his business and amusements. But there remain two facts that constitute a revolution. In the first place, conditions are such that this action is a matter of personal choice and resolution on the part of individuals, not of the very nature of social organization. In the second place, the very fact that an individual imports or carries his personal attitude into affairs that are inherently secular, that are outside the scope of religion, constitutes an enormous change, in spite of the belief that secular matters *should* be permeated by the spirit of religion. Even if it be asserted, as it is by some religionists, that all the new movements and interests of any value grew up under the auspices of a church and received their impetus from the same source, it must be admitted that once the vessels have been launched, they are sailing on strange seas to far lands.

Here, it seems to me, is the issue to be faced. Here is the place where the distinction that I have drawn between a religion and the religious function is peculiarly applicable. It is of the nature of a religion based on the supernatural to draw a line between the religious and the secular and profane, even when it asserts the rightful authority of the Church and its religion to dominate these other interests. The conception that "religious" signifies a certain attitude and outlook, independent of the supernatural, necessitates no such division. It does not shut religious values up within a particular compartment, nor assume that a particular form of association bears a unique relation to it. Upon the social side the future of the religious function seems preëminently bound up with its emancipation from religions and a particular religion. Many persons feel perplexed because of the multiplicity of churches and the conflict of their claims. But the fundamental difficulty goes deeper.

In what has been said I have not ignored the interpretation put, by representatives of religious organizations, upon the historic change that has occurred. The oldest organization, the Roman Catholic church, judges the secularization of life, the growing independence of social interests and values from control by the church, as but one evidence the more of the apostasy of the natural man from God: the corruption inherent in the will of mankind has resulted in defiance of the authority that God has delegated to his designated representatives on earth. This church points to the fact that secularization has proceeded *pari passu* with the extension of Protestantism as evidence of the wilful heresy of the latter in its appeal to private conscience and choice. The remedy is simple. Submission to the will of God, as continuously expressed through the organization that is his established vicegerent on earth, is the sole means by which social relations and values can again become coextensive with religion.

Protestant churches, on the contrary, have emphasized the fact that the relation of man to God is primarily an individual matter, a matter of personal choice and responsibility. From this point of view, one aspect of the change outlined marks an advance that is religious as well as moral. For according to it, the beliefs and rites that tend to make relation of man to God a collective and institutional affair erect barriers between the human soul and the divine spirit. Communion with God must be initiated by the individual's heart and will through direct divine assistance. Hence the change that has occurred in the social status of organized religion is nothing to deplore. What has been lost was at best specious and external. What has been gained is that religion has been placed upon its only real and solid foundation: direct relationship of conscience and will to God. Although there is much that is non-Christian and anti-Christian in existing economic and political institutions, it is better that change be accomplished by the sum total of efforts of men and women who are imbued with personal faith, than that they be effected by any wholesale institutional effort that subordinates the individual to an external and ultimately a worldly authority.

Were the question involved in these two opposed views taken up in detail, there are some specific considerations that might be urged. It might be urged that the progressive secularization of the interests of life has not been attended by the increasing degeneration that the argument of the first group implies. There are many who, as historical students, independent of affiliation with any religion, would regard reversal of the process of secularization and return to conditions in which the Church was the final authority as a menace to things held most precious. With reference to the position of Protestantism, it may be urged that in fact such social advances as have taken place are not the product of voluntary religious associations; that, on the contrary, the forces that have worked to humanize human relations, that have resulted in intellectual and æsthetic development, have come from influences that are independent of the churches. A case could be made out for the position that the churches have lagged behind in most important social movements and that they have turned their chief attention in social affairs to moral *symptoms*, to vices and abuses, like drunkenness, sale of intoxicants, divorce, rather than to the causes of war and of the long list of economic and political injustices and oppressions. Protest against the latter has been mainly left to secular movements.

In earlier times, what we now call the supernatural hardly meant anything more definite than the extraordinary, that which was striking and emotionally impressive because of its out-of-the-way character. Probably even today the commonest conception of the natural is that which is usual, customary and familiar. When there is no insight into the cause of unusual events, belief in the supernatural is itself "natural"—in this sense of natural. Supernaturalism was, therefore, a genuinely social religion as long as men's minds were attuned to the supernatural. It gave an "explanation" of extraordinary occurrences while it provided techniques for utilizing supernatural forces to secure advantages and to protect the members of the community against them when they were adverse.

The growth of natural science brought extraordinary things into line with events for which there is a "natural" explanation. At the same time, the development of positive social interests crowded heaven—and its opposite, hell—into the background. The function and offices of churches became more and more specialized; concerns and values that had been regarded, in an earlier contrast, as profane and secular grew in bulk and in importance. At the same time, the notion that basic and ultimate spiritual and ideal values are associated with the supernatural has persisted as a kind of vague background and aura. A kind of polite deference to the notion remains along with a concrete transfer of interest. The general mind is thus left in a confused and divided state. The movement that has been going on for the last few centuries will continue to breed doubleness of mind until religious meanings and values are definitely integrated into normal social relations.

The issue may be more definitely stated. The extreme position on one side is that apart from relation to the supernatural, man is morally on a level with the brutes. The other position is that all significant ends and all securities for stability and peace have grown up in the matrix of human relations, and that the values given a supernatural locus are in fact products of an idealizing imagination that has laid hold of natural goods. There ensues a second contrast. On the one hand, it is held that relation to the supernatural is the only finally dependable source of motive power; that directly and indirectly it has animated every serious effort for the guidance and rectification of man's life on earth. The other position is that goods actually experienced in the concrete relations of family, neighborhood, citizenship, pursuit of art and science, are what men actually depend upon for guidance and support, and that their reference to a supernatural and other-worldly locus has obscured their real nature and has weakened their force.

The contrasts outlined define the religious problem of the present and the future. What would be the consequences upon the values of human association if intrinsic and immanent satisfactions and opportunities were clearly held to and cultivated with the ardor and the devotion that have at times marked historic religions? The contention of an increasing number of persons is that depreciation of natural social values has resulted, both in principle and in actual fact, from reference of their origin and significance to supernatural sources. Natural relations, of husband and wife, of parent and child, friend and friend, neighbor and neighbor, of fellow workers in industry, science, and art, are neglected, passed over, not developed for all that is in them. They are, moreover, not merely depreciated. They have been regarded as dangerous rivals of higher values; as offering temptations to be resisted; as usurpations by flesh of the authority of the spirit; as revolts of the human against the divine.

The doctrine of original sin and total depravity, of the corruption of nature, external and internal, is not especially current in liberal religious circles at present. Rather, there prevails the idea that there are two separate systems of values—an idea similar to that referred to in the previous chapter about a revelation of two kinds of truth. The values found in natural and supernatural relationships are now, in liberal circles, said to be complementary, just as the truths of revelation and of science are the two sides, mutually sustaining, of the same ultimate truth.

I cannot but think that this position represents a great advance upon the traditional one. While it is open logically to the objections that hold against the idea of the dual revelation of truth, practically it indicates a development of a humane point of view. But if it be once admitted that human relations are charged with values that are religious in function, why not rest the case upon what is verifiable and concentrate thought and energy upon its full realization?

History seems to exhibit three stages of growth. In the first stage, human relationships were thought to be so infected with the evils of corrupt human nature as to require redemption from external and supernatural sources. In the next stage, what is significant in these relations is found to be akin to values esteemed distinctively religious. This is the point now reached by liberal theologians. The third stage would realize that in fact the values prized in those religions that have ideal elements are idealizations of things characteristic of natural association, which have then been projected into a supernatural realm for safe-keeping and sanction. Note the rôle of such terms as Father, Son, Bride, Fellowship and Communion in the vocabulary of Christianity, and note also the tendency, even if a somewhat inchoate one, of terms that express the more intimate phases of association to displace those of legal, political origin: King, Judge, and Lord of Hosts.

Unless there is a movement into what I have called the third stage, fundamental dualism and a division in life continue. The idea of a double and parallel manifestation of the divine, in which the latter has superior status and authority, brings about a condition of unstable equilibrium. It operates to distract energy, through dividing the objects to which it is directed. It also imperatively raises the question as to why having gone far in recognition of religious values in normal community life, we should not go further. The values of natural human intercourse and mutual dependence are open and public, capable of verification by the methods through which all natural facts are established. By means of the same experimental method, they are capable of expansion. Why not concentrate upon nurturing and extending them? Unless we take this step, the idea of two realms of spiritual values is only a softened version of the old dualism between the secular and the spiritual, the profane and the religious.

The condition of unstable equilibrium is indeed so evident to the thoughtful mind that there are attempts just now to revert to the earlier stage of belief. It is not difficult to make a severe indictment of existing social relations. It is enough to point to the war, jealousy, and fear that dominate the relations of national states to one another; to the growing demoralization of the older ties of domestic life; to the staggering evidence of corruption and futility in politics, and to the egoism, brutality, and oppression that characterize economic activities. By piling up material of this sort, one may, if one chooses, arrive at the triumphant conclusion that social relations are so debased that the only recourse is to supernatural aid. The general disorder of the Great War and succeeding decades has led to a revival of the theology of corruption, sin, and need for supernatural redemption.

The conclusion does not follow, however, from the data. It ignores, in the first place, that all the positive values which are prized, and in aid of which supernatural power is appealed to, have, after all, emerged from the very scene of human associations of which it is possible to paint so black a picture. Something in the facts has been left out of the picture. I shall not bring forward again at this place what was earlier said as to the effect upon actual conditions of diversion of the thought and action of those who are peculiarly sensitive to ideal considerations into supernatural channels. I shall raise a more directly practical issue. Society is convicted of being "immoral" by evoking all the evils of institutions as they now exist, and the unexpressed premise is that the institutions as they exist are normal expressions of social relations in their own nature.

Were this premise stated, the enormous gap between it and the conclusion set forth would be apparent. The problem of the relation between social relations and institutions that are dominant at a particular time is the most intricate problem presented to social inquiry. The idea that the latter are a direct reflex of the former ignores the multiplicity of factors that historically have entered into the shaping of institutions. Historically speaking, many of these factors are accidental with respect to the institutional form that has been given to social relations. One of my favorite quotations is a statement of Clarence Ayers that "our industrial revolution began, as some historians say, with half a dozen technical improvements in the textile industry; and it took us a century to realize that anything of moment had happened to us, beyond the obvious improvement of spinning and weaving." This statement must serve in lieu of long argument to suggest what I mean by the "accidental" relation of institutional developments to the primary facts of human association. The relation is accidental because institutional consequences that have resulted were not foreseen or intended. To say this, is to say that social intelligence in the sense in which there is intelligence about physical relations is in so far nonexistent.

Here is the negative fact that renders argument for the necessity of supernatural intervention to effect significant betterment only just another instance of the old, old inference to the supernatural from the basis of ignorance. We lack, for example, knowledge of the relation of life to inanimate matter. Therefore supernatural intervention is assumed to have effected the transition from brute to man. We do not know the relation of the organism—the brain and nervous system—to the occurrence of thought. Therefore, it is argued, there is a supernatural link. We do not know the relation of causes to results in social matters, and consequently we lack means of control. Therefore, it is inferred, we must resort to supernatural control. Of course, I make no claim to knowing how far intelligence may and will develop in respect to social relations. But one thing I think I do know. The needed understanding will not develop unless we strive for it. The assumption that only supernatural agencies can give control is a sure method of retarding this effort. It is as sure to be a hindering force now with respect to social intelligence, as the similar appeal was earlier an obstruction in the development of physical knowledge.

Even immediately, without awaiting the development of greater intelligence in relation to social affairs, a great difference would be made by use of natural means and methods. It is even now possible to examine complex social phenomena sufficiently to put the finger on things that are wrong. It is possible to trace to some extent these evils to their causes, and to causes that are something very different from abstract moral forces. It is possible to work out and work upon remedies for some of the sore spots. The outcome will not be a gospel of salvation but it will be in line with that pursued, for example, in matters of disease and health. The method if used would not only accomplish something toward social health but it would accomplish a greater thing; it would forward the development of social intelligence so that it could act with greater hardihood and on a larger scale.

Vested interests, interests vested with power, are powerfully on the side of the *status quo,* and therefore they are especially powerful in hindering the growth and application of the method of natural intelligence. Just because these interests are so powerful, it is the more necessary to fight for recognition of the method of intelligence in action. But one of the greatest obstacles in conducting this combat is the tendency to dispose of social evils in terms of general moral causes. The sinfulness of man, the corruption of his heart, his self-love and love of power, when referred to as causes are precisely of the same nature as was the appeal to abstract powers (which in fact only reduplicated under a general name a multitude of particular effects) that once prevailed in physical "science," and that operated as a chief obstacle to the generation and growth of the latter. Demons were once appealed to in order to explain bodily disease and no such thing as a strictly natural death was supposed to happen. The importation of general moral causes to explain present *social* phenomena is on the same intellectual level. Reinforced by the prestige of traditional religions, and backed by the emotional force of beliefs in the supernatural, it stifles the growth of that social intelligence by means of which direction of social change could be taken out of the region of accident, as accident has been defined. Accident in this broad sense and the idea of the supernatural are twins. Interest in the supernatural therefore reinforces other vested interests to prolong the social reign of accident.

There is a strong reaction in some religious circles today against the idea of mere individual salvation of individual souls. There is also a reaction in politics and economics against the idea of *laissez faire*. Both of these movements reflect a common tendency. Both of them are signs of the growing awareness of the emptiness of individuality in isolation. But the fundamental root of the *laissez faire* idea is denial (more often implicit than express) of the possibility of radical intervention of intelligence in the conduct of human life. Now appeal for supernatural intervention in improvement of social matters is also the expression of a deep-seated *laissez-faireism*; it is the acknowledgment of the desperate situation into which we are driven by the idea of the irrelevance and futility of human intervention in social events and interests. Those contemporary theologians who are interested in social change and who at the same time depreciate human intelligence and effort in behalf of the supernatural, are riding two horses that are going in opposite directions. The old-fashioned ideas of doing something to make the will of God prevail in the world, and of assuming the responsibility of doing the job ourselves, have more to be said for them, logically and practically.

The emphasis that has been put upon intelligence as a method should not mislead anyone. Intelligence, as distinct from the older conception of reason, is inherently involved in action. Moreover, there is no opposition between it and emotion. There is such a thing as passionate intelligence, as ardor in behalf of light shining into the murky places of social existence, and as zeal for its refreshing and purifying effect. The whole story of man shows that there are no objects that may not deeply stir engrossing emotion. One of the few experiments in the attachment of emotion to ends that mankind has not tried is that of devotion, so intense as to be religious, to intelligence as a force in social action.

But this is only part of the scene. No matter how much evidence may be piled up against social institutions as they exist, affection and passionate desire for justice and security are realities in human nature. So are the emotions that arise from living in conditions of inequity, oppression, and insecurity. Combination of the two kinds of emotion has more than once produced those changes that go by the

name of revolution. To say that emotions which are
not fused with intelligence are blind is tautology.
Intense emotion may utter itself in action that de-
stroys institutions. But the only assurance of birth
of better ones is the marriage of emotion with intelligence.

Criticism of the commitment of religion to the
supernatural is thus positive in import. All modes
of human association are "affected with a public interest," and full realization of this interest is equivalent to a sense of a significance that is religious in
its function. The objection to supernaturalism is
that it stands in the way of an effective realization
of the sweep and depth of the implications of natural human relations. It stands in the way of using
the means that are in our power to make radical
changes in these relations. It is certainly true that
great material changes might be made with no corresponding improvement of a spiritual or ideal nature. But development in the latter direction cannot
be introduced from without; it cannot be brought
about by dressing up material and economic changes
with decorations derived from the supernatural. It
can come only from more intense realization of values
that inhere in the actual connections of human beings
with one another. The attempt to segregate the implicit public interest and social value of all institutions and social arrangements in a particular organization is a fatal diversion.

Were men and women actuated throughout the
length and breadth of human relations with the faith

and ardor that have at times marked historic religions
the consequences would be incalculable. To achieve
this faith and *élan* is no easy task. But religions have
attempted something similar, directed moreover
toward a less promising object—the supernatural.
It does not become those who hold that faith may
move mountains to deny in advance the possibility of
its manifestation on the basis of verifiable realities.
There already exists, though in a rudimentary form,
the capacity to relate social conditions and events to
their causes, and the ability will grow with exercise.
There is the technical skill with which to initiate a
campaign for social health and sanity analogous to
that made in behalf of physical public health.
Human beings have impulses toward affection, com-
passion and justice, equality and freedom. It remains
to weld all these things together. It is of no use
merely to assert that the intrenched foes of class interest and power in high places are hostile to the
realization of such a union. As I have already said,
if this enemy did not exist, there would be little
sense in urging *any* policy of change. The point to
be grasped is that, unless one gives up the whole
struggle as hopeless, one has to choose between alternatives. One alternative is dependence upon the
supernatural; the other, the use of natural agencies.

There is then no sense, logical or practical, in
pointing out the difficulties that stand in the way of
the latter course, until the question of the alternative
is faced. If it is faced, it will also be realized that
one factor in the choice is dependence upon enlisting

only those committed to the supernatural and alliance with all men and women who feel the stir of social emotion, including the large number of those who, consciously or unconsciously, have turned their backs upon the supernatural. Those who face the alternatives will also have to choose between a continued and even more systematic *laissez faire* depreciation of intelligence and the resources of natural knowledge and understanding, and conscious and organized effort to turn the use of these means from narrow ends, personal and class, to larger human purposes. They will have to ask, as far as they nominally believe in the need for radical social change, whether what they accomplish when they point with one hand to the seriousness of present evils is not undone when the other hand points away from man and nature for their remedy.

The transfer of idealizing imagination, thought and emotion to natural human relations would not signify the destruction of churches that now exist. It would rather offer the means for a recovery of vitality. The fund of human values that are prized and that need to be cherished, values that are satisfied and rectified by *all* human concerns and arrangements, could be celebrated and reinforced, in different ways and with differing symbols, by the churches. In that way the churches would indeed become catholic. The demand that churches show a more active interest in social affairs, that they take a definite stand upon such questions as war, economic injustice, political corruption, that they stimulate action for a divine kingdom on earth, is one of the signs of the times. But as long as social values are related to a supernatural for which the churches stand in some peculiar way, there is an inherent inconsistency between the demand and efforts to execute it. On the one hand, it is urged that the churches are going outside their special province when they involve themselves in economic and political issues. On the other hand, the very fact that they claim if not a monopoly of supreme values and motivating forces, yet a unique relation to them, makes it impossible for the churches to participate in promotion of social ends on a natural and equal human basis. The surrender of claims to an exclusive and authoritative position is a *sine qua non* for doing away with the dilemma in which churches now find themselves in respect to their sphere of social action.

At the outset, I referred to an outstanding historic fact. The coincidence of the realm of social interests and activities with a tribal or civic community has vanished. Secular interests and activities have grown up outside of organized religions and are independent of their authority. The hold of these interests upon the thoughts and desires of men has crowded the social importance of organized religions into a corner and the area of this corner is decreasing. This change either marks a terrible decline in everything that can justly be termed religious in value, in traditional religions, or it provides the opportunity for expansion of these qualities on a new basis and with a new outlook. It is impossible to ignore the fact that historic Christianity has been committed to a separation of sheep and goats; the saved and the lost; the elect and the mass. Spiritual aristocracy as well as *laissez faire* with respect to natural and human intervention, is deeply embedded in its traditions. Lip service—often more than lip service—has been given to the idea of the common brotherhood of all men. But those outside the fold of the church and those who do not rely upon belief in the supernatural have been regarded as only potential brothers, still requiring adoption into the family. I cannot understand how any realization of the democratic ideal as a vital moral and spiritual ideal in human affairs is possible without surrender of the conception of the basic division to which supernatural Christianity is committed. Whether or no we are, save in some metaphorical sense, all brothers, we are at least all in the same boat traversing the same turbulent ocean. The potential religious significance of this fact is infinite.

In the opening chapter I made a distinction between religion and the religious. I pointed out that religion—or religions—is charged with beliefs, practices and modes of organization that have accrued to and been loaded upon the religious element in experience by the state of culture in which religions have developed. I urged that conditions are now ripe for emancipation of the religious quality from accretions that have grown up about it and that limit the credibility and the influence of religion. In the second chapter, I developed this idea with respect to the faith in ideals that is immanent in the religious value of experience, and asserted that the power of this faith would be enhanced were belief freed from the conception that the significance and validity of the ideal are bound up with intellectual assent to the proposition that the ideal is already embodied in some supernatural or metaphysical sense in the very framework of existence.

The matter touched upon in the present chapter includes within itself all that has been previously set forth. It does so upon both its negative and positive sides. The community of causes and consequences in which we, together with those not born, are enmeshed is the widest and deepest symbol of the mysterious totality of being the imagination calls the universe. It is the embodiment for sense and thought of that encompassing scope of existence the intellect cannot grasp. It is the matrix within which our ideal aspirations are born and bred. It is the source of the values that the moral imagination projects as directive criteria and as shaping purposes.

The continuing life of this comprehensive community of beings includes all the significant achievement of men in science and art and all the kindly offices of intercourse and communication. It holds within its content all the material that gives verifiable intellectual support to our ideal faiths. A "creed" founded on this material will change and grow, but it cannot be shaken. What it surrenders it gives up gladly because of new light and not as a reluctant concession. What it adds, it adds because new knowledge gives further insight into the conditions that bear upon the formation and execution of our life purposes. A one-sided psychology, a reflex of eighteenth-century "individualism," treated knowledge as an accomplishment of a lonely mind. We should now be aware that it is a product of the cooperative and communicative operations of human beings living together. Its communal origin is an indication of its rightful communal use. The unification of what is known at any given time, not upon an impossible eternal and abstract basis but upon that of its bearing upon the unification of human desire and purpose, furnishes a sufficient creed for human acceptance, one that would provide a religious release and reinforcement of knowledge.

"Agnosticism" is a shadow cast by the eclipse of the supernatural. Of course, acknowledgment that we do not know what we do not know is a necessity of all intellectual integrity. But generalized agnosticism is only a halfway elimination of the supernatural. Its meaning departs when the intellectual outlook is directed wholly to the natural world. When it is so directed, there are plenty of particular matters regarding which we must say we do not know; we only inquire and form hypotheses which future inquiry will confirm or reject. But such doubts are an incident of faith in the method of intelligence. They are signs of faith, not of a pale and impotent skepticism. We doubt in order that we may find out, not because some inaccessible supernatural lurks behind whatever *we* can know. The substantial background of practical faith in ideal ends is positive and out-reaching.

The considerations put forward in the present chapter may be summed up in what they imply. The ideal ends to which we attach our faith are not shadowy and wavering. They assume concrete form in our understanding of our relations to one another and the values contained in these relations. We who now live are parts of a humanity that extends into the remote past, a humanity that has interacted with nature. The things in civilization we most prize are not of ourselves. They exist by grace of the doings and sufferings of the continuous human community in which we are a link. Ours is the responsibility of conserving, transmitting, rectifying and expanding the heritage of values we have received that those who come after us may receive it more solid and secure, more widely accessible and more generously shared than we have received it. Here are all the elements for a religious faith that shall not be confined to sect, class, or race. Such a faith has always been implicitly the common faith of mankind. It remains to make it explicit and militant.

BOOKS PUBLISHED
BY
FREDERICK ELLIS
(New Hardbacks)

Buy Direct - 25% Off
Free Shipping - Pay with PayPal

Contact - frederick659@yahoo.com

Author - Jack London

$43.75............MARTIN EDEN

$36.75..............WAR OF THE CLASSES

$36.75............JOHN BARLEYCORN

$33.75............THE PEOPLE OF THE ABYSS

$34.75..............JACK LONDON ON THE ROAD

$35.75............THE ASSASSINATION BUREAU, LTD.

$36.75..............THE IRON HEEL

Author - Bruno Traven

$32.75............GENERAL FROM THE JUNGLE

$38.75..............THE DEATH SHIP

$35.75..............THE REBELLION OF THE HANGED

$34.75..............THE WHITE ROSE

$34.75..............THE BRIDGE IN THE JUNGLE

$34.75..............MARCH TO THE MONTERIA

$37.95..............THE TREASURE OF THE SIERRA MADRE

Author – Carl Frederick

$39.95...............est: PLAYING THE GAME THE NEW WAY

Authors - Frederick Ellis & Carl Frederick

$19.75................THE OAKLAND STATEMENT (softcover)

Author – Mao Tsetung

$39.75...............QUOTATIONS FROM CHAIRMAN MAO TSETUNG

Author – Upton Sinclair

$33.75...............OUR LADY

$44.75................OIL

$39.75................THE JUNGLE

$32.75................THE FLIVVER KING: THE STORY OF FORD-AMERICA

$35.75................ONE HUNDRED PERCENT: THE STORY OF A PATRIOT

$37,75................WORLD'S END I

$42.75................WORLD'S END II

$34.75................THE SECRET LIFE OF JESUS

$34.75................THE MONEYCHANGERS

$35.75................MENTAL RADIO

$35.75................THE MILLENIUM

$35.75................A PERSONAL JESUS

$36.75................PROFITS OF RELIGION

$34.95................THEY CALL ME CARPENTER: A TALE OF
THE SECOND COMING

$45.75................DRAGON'S TEETH

Author – Thomas Paine

$38.75................COMMON SENSE & THE RIGHTS OF MAN
& THE AGE OF REASON

$33.75................THE AMERICAN CRISIS

Author – Karl Marx

$39.75................DAS KAPITAL

$33.75................THE COMMUNIST MANIFESTO &
WAGES, PRICE AND PROFIT

$32.75................WAGE-LABOUR AND CAPITAL
& VALUE, PRICE AND PROFIT

Author – W. E. B. Du Bois

$34.75................THE SOULS OF BLACK FOLK

Author – Eugene Debs

$35.75................WALLS AND BARS

Author – Jean-Jacques Rousseau

$34.75................THE SOCIAL CONTRACT

Author – John Reed

$37.75..................TEN DAYS THAT SHOOK THE WORLD

$36.75..................INSURGENT MEXICO

Author – Antonio Gramsci

$33.75..................THE MODERN PRINCE AND
SELECTED WRITINGS

Author – V. I. Lenin

$35.75..................THE STATE AND REVOLUTION

$36.95..................FIGHT AGAINST STALINISM & IMPERIALISM: THE HIGHEST STAGE
OF CAPITALISM

Author – John Dewey

$35.75....................HOW WE THINK & EDUCATION AND EXPERIENCE

$37.75.................. INDIVIDUALISM OLD AND NEW & LIBERALISM AND SOCIAL
ACTION & A COMMON FAITH

$39.75..................DEMOCRACY AND EDUCATION & FREEDOM AND CULTURE

Author – David Ricardo

$37.75....................PRINCIPLES OF POLITICAL ECONOMY
AND TAXATION

4

Author – Thomas Jefferson

$34.75................BIOGRAPHY OF THOMAS JEFFERSON & THE LIFE AND MORALS OF JESUS OF NAZARETH

Author – Emma Goldman

$35.95................ANARCHISM AND OTHER WRITINGS

Author – Rosa Luxemburg

$32.95................REFORM OR REVOLUTION & THE MASS STRIKE

Author – Leon Trotsky

$35.75................THE REVOLUTION BETRAYED

Author – John Stuart Mill

$33.95................ON SOCIALISM & THE SUBJECTION OF WOMEN

Author – Friedrich Nietzsche

$34.75................BEYOND GOOD AND EVIL

$40.75................THE BIRTH OF TRAGEDY & 75 APHORISMS & THE ANTI-CHRIST

Author – John Quincy Adams

$33.95................THE AMISTAD ARGUMENT & THE STATE OF THE UNION ADDRESSES

Authors – James Madison. Alexander Hamilton, John Jay

$40.75................THE FEDERALIST PAPERS

5

www.ingramcontent.com/pod-product-compliance
Lightning Source LLC
Chambersburg PA
CBHW020402100426
42812CB00001B/172